WHAT ALL LITTLE GIRLS *need* & WHAT MOST WOMEN *never had*

"Healthy, Loving Relationships with Their Fathers"

Joe Cucchiara

Tate Publishing, LLC

I dedicate this book to my two beautiful, loving, smart, and talented daughters, Rachel and Stephanie.

They have inspired my passionate awareness and vision for recognizing the importance of healthy, loving relationships between fathers and daughters.

TABLE OF CONTENTS

Introduction
CHAPTER 1 15
   Commitment 15
   Make a Pact.. 18
   Priorities 19
   Design your Relationship 21
   Newborn Love.. 23
   Create a Bond 25
CHAPTER 2 27
   Trust and Respect 27
   Be Involved 29
   Teach with Patience.................................... 31
   A Mind of Her Own 33
   No One is Perfect.. 36
   Let Her Teach You 38
CHAPTER 3 43
   School and Education................................... 43
   What a formal education won't teach her 45
CHAPTER 4 49
   Eating Habits and Body Image 49
   Sports, Exercise, and Physical Activities 53
   Religion and Spirituality............................ 58
CHAPTER 5 63
   "Daddy, play with us." 63
   Games We Play.. 65
   Cooking, Baking, Cleaning, and Laundry . 69
CHAPTER 6 73
   Same-Page Parenting 73
   Embrace Family Structure 75
   SLOW DOWN! 79

Structure and Discipline............................ 84
Rituals and Routines................................. 93
Work-Life Balance 96
CHAPTER 7... 99
Words and Actions—Choose Wisely......... 99
Be a Role Model 102
No Stereotypes 104
Real Equality   107
A Father's View 112
CHAPTER 8... 117
Abuse.. 117
The Facts 120
Sex Education, Smoking, Drugs,
and Alcohol.. 126
CHAPTER 9... 135
Rebuild your Relationship...................... 135
You're the only father your
daughter will ever have!........................ 139

INTRODUCTION

What have your grandfathers and father's relationships been like with their daughters? More specifically, what was your grandfather's relationship like with your mother? What was your father's relationship like with your mother and any sisters you have? As a man or father, what effect have those past-generational relationships had on your past or present relationships with girls and women, including your daughter? Do you find it easier to relate and connect with your son than with your daughter? If so, why is that? Would you consider your current relationship with your daughter to be healthy, loving, fulfilling, and free of stereotypes? How do you really know if you're on the right path, and how and where does a father start?

These are crucial questions we should be asking ourselves if we want to avoid some of the mistakes our grandfathers and fathers made in raising daughters and how they treated both girls and women in general. If our daughters are important to us, we have a chance to be the first generation to make a major difference in the way we raise them and the way men perceive girls and women.

In the past, many of our grandmothers, mothers, and daughters were raised with serious gender stereotypes that discouraged independence, education, and self-worth. Well, here we are in the 21st century, and many young girls and women in our generation still face the same challenges. As fathers, if we want things to change for our young daughters in the world at large—for them to be treated equally, to be granted the same opportunities as boys, and to be raised free of stereotypes—we must join together to make some changes ourselves—changes in the way we raise our own daughters.

Both of my grandfathers had nonexistent, dysfunctional relationships with their wives and daughters. My father had a similar relationship with my mother and all three of his daughters, my sisters. In fact, in my family there were numerous forms of abuse, which included sexual abuse, emotional abuse, and verbal abuse, as well as outright neglect. This pattern was repeated on both sides of my family for generations. Our father was an alcoholic and drug user, a man who had no respect for girls and women. Our mother was a codependent enabler in their parental relationship. Sadly, both of my parents and their parents were raised in a similar environment. It wasn't until I was in my twenties and in a serious relationship that I realized the emotional and psychological challenges I was faced with because of what I had been exposed to while growing up. I had no idea what a healthy, fulfilling relationship between a man and a woman felt and looked like. I was preconditioned to fail by duplicating the unhealthy, abusive relationships I witnessed as a child.

In my twenties, still seeing the same girl, Synthia, who later became my wife, I experienced years of mood swings, frustration, and self-sabotage. I didn't like the way I was feeling, but had no idea why I felt that way. I became a master at avoiding my inner emotions by working more and more hours, trying to find reasons why the relationship wasn't working. Finally, I reached a point where I didn't like the way I was acting and reacting with my girlfriend and how it was affecting my life, so I decided to get help.

I sought professional counseling to help deal with the challenges and frustrations in my relationship, and it turned out to be one of the best things I could have done. I realized that I wasn't alone, and that there were a number of reasons why I was experiencing these challenges. During my initial sessions, my therapist explained to me that my actions and reactions were common traits found in children raised in alcoholic or abusive families. After spending time seeking help, educating myself, and trying hard to understand my past, I started generating positive results in my relationships. The past ten years or so have been much easier for me, but they've continued to include hard work, occasional tune-ups, and follow-up visits with my therapist. My next challenge and cause for anxiety came when my wife and I decided to have our first child.

I was overwhelmed with joy and love when we had our first, beautiful, little girl, Rachel. However, knowing what I had gone through in the past, as well as the failures of my parents and their parents, the last thing I wanted to do was repeat the pattern of dysfunctional parental behavior. At that point in my life, I made a commitment to my wife and child to be a caring, loving, and participating father. I also vowed to raise my daughter without stereotypes, providing her with equal opportunities to learn and excel in life regardless of her gender. These commitments were the result of my effort and dedication to distinguish healthy from unhealthy relationships between men and women. It was critical that I understood how important it was to build a healthy and loving relationship with my wife and daughter.

Many girls grow up, seek out, and attract the attention of the wrong men, for the wrong reasons. In addition, many girls also grow up without their own identities, a sense of independence, or the resolve to achieve personal and professional goals. One of the most common reasons many girls grow up this way is that they lack healthy, loving relationships with their fathers, free of gender bias. A loving relationship includes total commitment and involvement in your daughter's life from the time she's born until the time she leaves the house and beyond. Unfortunately, many men still feel awkward and uncomfortable developing loving and intimate relationships with their young daughters and have a very difficult time bonding, interacting, and relating to them.

I wrote this book with the hope that men, either by themselves or through help from others, could understand the importance of developing healthy, loving relationships with their young daughters. In addition, my desire is for people to see that I myself had to make a choice, either to continue the generational pattern of dysfunction or to create a new path for my daughters. The truth is that most people are faced with these very same challenges; the exciting part is that they, too, are capable of making positive changes.

While reading this book, you may find that

much of my philosophy is nontraditional, and I have taken a nonstereotypical approach in developing healthy, loving relationships with my young daughters. I am happy to say I have experienced a tremendous amount of success and joy following this path and have already been rewarded with a host of wonderful memories.

I have two amazing and loving daughters, whom I am extremely proud of and love dearly. At the time of this writing, Rachel is eleven years old; Stephanie is eight years old. Over the past eleven years, I have developed a passionate philosophy about parenting and a lifelong commitment to being a loving and involved father for my daughters. Because of this passion and commitment, I have spent several years of research in this area. However, one of the most unique and compelling facets of my experience and journey has been the coinciding relationships and time spent with other women and young girls in my family, neighborhood, church, and work.

I was raised with three sisters, and my mother has six sisters in her family. My wife, Synthia, has six sisters. I managed a customer service department for over ten years; of the thirty-five employees, thirty were women. Finally, for the past ten years I have lived in a wonderful neighborhood with families that boast roughly seventeen girls under the age of twenty-one. You can see, girls and women have played a major role in my life thus far and have provided plenty of resources and experiences from which to draw. Between my wife's family and mine, there are approximately thirty girls and women who have had dysfunctional, nonexistent, or unhealthy relationships with their fathers. Because of this, many of the women in our two families have made poor choices in the men they have dated or have married. In addition to our two families, I know countless other women that fit this same category. What can fathers do to change this damaging and tragic pattern? As you'll discover in this book, we must make our daughters a priority in our lives and commit to taking the necessary time and steps to develop and maintain healthy, loving relationships with them. When you've finished reading this book, please share your thoughts and feelings with your daughters and make a commitment, no matter what their ages. Never forget, you're the only father your daughter will ever have.

To the girls and women reading this book, I encourage you to use it as a resource for exploring and helping in the following areas of your life: First, use it to learn more about your relationship with your father and its effect on your life, past or present. Second, use it to help improve your current relationship with your father. Third, married women, use it to assist your husbands in improving and strengthening their relationships with their daughters.

We get only one chance to raise our daughters, and most of us would like to do the best job we can, with the best resources at our disposal. This book offers men a simple and easy-to-understand approach to raising their young daughters. In addition, it provides many creative ideas and suggestions on how to better develop healthy, loving relationships with them. It also gives girls and women the unique opportunity to explore what many of them missed out on and what every little girl needs and deserves from her father.

Always remember this: There is a very good chance that a daughter will grow up to date and marry a man similar to her father. Most likely, she will also allow men to talk to her and treat her the way her father talked to and treated her and her mother. So just how important do you think a healthy, loving relationship is between a father and his daughter? **You decide.**

CHAPTER 1
Commitment

Like anything else in life, if we are serious about making a positive difference, we must make a commitment and stick to it. Therefore, the first step men should take in improving and developing a healthy, loving relationship with their young daughters is to make a serious commitment and remain accountable to it.

Chances are that this commitment and change will not come naturally or easily. Please be prepared for the possibility that you'll get off track from time to time and fall back into some of your old habits and patterns. If and when this happens, remain strong and work hard at getting right back on track. If married, I strongly suggest that you involve your spouse and daughter; allow them to help you stay accountable. This could be difficult at times, because we don't always like to be reminded when we fail to live up to our commitment. However, please don't let your pride and stubbornness get in the way of your journey. Seek professional help if you are really struggling. Read as much material as you can about this topic and talk with other people facing the same challenges and see how they have stayed the course.

One thing I found very helpful for myself is to post a list of what I call "Priorities in Life." I always try to keep that list visible. By posting a list of my life priorities at the location where I spend most of my time, it acts as a constant reminder.

After a while, even if you don't look at this list every day, you will still know it's there. One wonderful reward is to post your priorities where your daughter and other family members will also see them. Remember, reinforcement is the key. Also, try to find friends or family members who respect what you're doing and use them as a sounding board. Those who truly care for you and support what you're trying to accomplish will be happy to talk with you and help in any way they can.

Another issue to be aware of is how others around you may react to your commitment and dedication. Any time you change or make positive adjustments in your life, you'll be faced with people who are uncomfortable with these changes. Many people don't understand what it means or what it takes to make positive change and are often critical and judgmental of your new journey. Most of the time, this occurs because these people are insecure about areas of their own lives. Maybe these same people have continued to receive validation of their own insecurities from you to some extent in the past, when your lifestyle and habits were similar to theirs.

Once you begin to make changes, these people will likely act out in a number of different ways. They might challenge the *new* you. They might accuse you of acting as if you're too good for them or not being one of the guys anymore or of any number of things. These people might even be family members or good friends. Whatever you do, please don't let these potentially negative forces get in the way of your commitment to becoming a better person and father for your daughter. If you have to, remove yourself from people who do not support and embrace your commitment. At least limit the time you spend with them. To make positive change, you must remove yourself from past and present harmful relationships. Whether they are family or friends, you can't afford to expose yourself or your young daughter to those negative associations if you expect to become a better person and father to her.

Look around and observe family, friends, and neighbors to see what kinds of relationships they have with their daughters. Watch their interaction and see how other fathers and daughters relate to each other. If you see what appears to be a healthy, bonding, and respectful relationship, talk with those fathers and ask questions about what works for them. You can always learn from others to be a better person and father. Sit down with your daughter when she is about four years old and ask her what she likes best about your relationship. Ask her what activities she enjoys most with you. Ask her if there is anything else she would like the two of you to do together. You'll be surprised at how clear your daughter can be about her needs and wants. Trust her opinion and listen to what she has to say. Whatever you do, please don't doubt or question what she likes or wants to do. Remember, your daughter shouldn't be making choices based on what makes you happy, but what makes her happy. Make a commitment to invest emotionally in the relationship, and it will develop into one you both will cherish forever.

Make a Pact

Once you have made your commitment to developing a healthy, loving relationship with your daughter, make sure she hears it from you, and remind her often. This is the foundation and the beginning of your emotional pact with her.

Too often we keep our commitments to ourselves and don't share them with the people who count the most and who can benefit the most by hearing our commitments. No matter what her age, make sure to tell your daughter over and over again how much you love her and how important she is to you. Tell her how happy you are to have her in your life. By expressing these types of wonderful things over and over, you will continue to emotionally validate your connection and love. Even more important, your daughter must always know in her heart that she can trust you and what you say.

A day should not go by without you telling your daughter how much you love her and how much she means to you. Please don't mistake the difference between personally telling her how you feel versus praising her for something she has done. Although both are very important, they are two entirely different things and have different meanings. For example, if you tell your daughter how proud you are of her for accomplishing something, the focus is on what she accomplished. If you tell your daughter how much you love her and how important she is to you, for no reason at all, the focus is on how you feel about her as a person. Your daughter needs to know that regardless of the circumstances you will always love her. If you only praise her when she accomplishes something, she will tend to feel that she needs to do something in order to please you.

Don't misunderstand me; it's natural for children to want to please their parents. However, our daughters shouldn't be raised feeling as if they must please us. As her father, talk to her about finding different things in life she might enjoy and that might make her happy. The sooner your daughter emotionally connects with you, the better chance you have to develop mutual trust and respect. Reinforce your pact and your love for your daughter by what you say and by what you do.

Priorities

The word priority gets thrown around a lot. When you draw up your list of priorities, I would make sure you sincerely consider what is more important to you and what will potentially have the most positive effects on your life. These priorities might include you and your spouse, your children, family members, friends, and career. Those of you with spiritual or religious beliefs should certainly add that to the top of your list as well.

I am very passionate about this topic and suggest that we fathers be honest with ourselves to be sure that we are *walking the talk*. For instance, I can't claim that my family is my top priority and the most important part of my life, yet continue to work twelve to fifteen hours a day for years and years. If I spend little time with my spouse and young daughters, what really is my top priority?

We have an epidemic today in our society where many men still fail to understand the importance of their participation and involvement in their daughters' lives. If you take this personally—and please do—do it for positive reasons. Let me explain why. All of us fathers should take something this important personally, and if we don't, we just don't care enough. I know, because I took this personally and had to ask myself these very same questions many years ago. Fortunately, I made my priority adjustments when my first daughter was born. I can tell you that it wasn't easy back then, and still, it is very difficult at times trying to balance my priorities.

However, if we don't address our true priorities as soon as possible, we will most likely regret it for years to come and maybe the rest of our lives. If this sounds harsh, it's because it is. This is a reality for millions of predominantly older men and women. Many of these people will tell you that there are primarily two things that they regret most. The first is not having established healthy, loving relationships with their spouses or children, and the second is not spending enough time with them early in life. So please take a serious look at your priorities right away, and work hard to make the adjustments sooner rather than later. To make a difference in your daughter's life and build a healthy, loving relationship with her, you first must make her a top priority.

Design your Relationship

Now that you have your commitment and priorities squared away, it's time to design and develop your relationship plan concerning you and your daughter. No, not your business plan, your relationship plan. I realize this might sound strange, and it is a different way of thinking, but stick with me on this one. Many of us spend many hours (if not days, weeks, months, and even years), if we're smart, planning for retirement. We also spend time planning our vacations, buying our vacation homes, and purchasing our new cars. We often spend time crafting and planning for a promotion, a career change, or a diet. As a matter of fact, many parents spend more time watching television every day than they spend with their children. However, many of us don't work at designing and planning relationships with our loved ones. Most of us are conditioned to think relationships take care of themselves. This couldn't be further from the truth, and it is where too many of us go wrong.

As soon as your daughter is born, or even before, take the time to write up a plan for how you would like your relationship with your daughter to develop over the years. For example, let's say your plan is to develop a healthy, loving relationship with your daughter from the time she's born through age thirteen. The next step would be to determine what your goals and objectives are and how you will meet or exceed them. This will take some time and creativity, so please try to have fun with it. Like most plans, the easy part is coming up with what you want and what your goals are. The difficult part is constructing and deploying an action plan to achieve these goals and having checks and balances along the way. Of course, the simplest way to develop your plan is to finish reading this book and use some or all of the material to assist you in crafting your plan. I recommend you start by jotting down your thoughts and taking notes in rough-draft form.

Start with a draft of how you would like to see your relationship develop and flourish over a period of time. Once you have your thoughts and your vision intact, begin to build a list of things you would like to do with your daughter, now and as she gets older. It's best to start at whatever age your daughter is currently and work your way through her teenage years.

Your plan might begin something like this:

During the first year of my daughter's life, I will spend a designated amount of time each day holding and playing with her as much as I can. I will help change her diapers, bathe her, and feed her. A day will not go by without me telling her how much I love her and how important she is to me. The second year I'll continue doing the same things I did the first year (which still apply). In addition, I'll read to my daughter at least once a day and take her to the park or out for a walk at least twice a week, etc.

Of course, every year you will add and adjust the items in your plan and on your list. As your daughter gets older, you will want to add time with her and age-appropriate activities that she enjoys. Be creative and innovative; expose her to new events, activities, educational issues, and sports. No matter what you add or delete from your annual list, every day you must continue to tell your daughter how much you love her and how important she is to you. Keep in mind, as with any plan, there are always adjustments required along the way. It is a work in progress, and most likely, there will be things that work and seem to fit and others that won't. Amend your plan with your daughter over the years, and encourage her to make suggestions and recommendations as well. Good luck and happy planning. Believe me, this will be one of the most important and fruitful plans you will ever develop.

Newborn Love

In case you haven't experienced it yet, there is nothing in the world more amazing and beautiful as a newborn baby. With all the technological wonders in the world and the most incredible achievements known to us, nothing is more beautiful or important as a new gift of life from God. This is where it all begins!

Please make sure you fully participate in your wife's pregnancy and your daughter's birth. Once your daughter is born, she'll naturally look to her parents for love. One of the most remarkable things about newborn babies is that they enter into life loving unconditionally and without emotional baggage, hidden agendas, and prejudices. Every chance we get, we should hold our newborn daughters, talk to them, sing to them, and show them that we love them.

While holding your daughter, she will feel a physical and emotional attachment that will help to develop a special bond between you and her. Much of this might sound simple and make sense to most people. Still, many times we get preoccupied with other areas of our lives and forget the importance of this time we should spend with our newborns. Often we can get into a pattern where the only time we hold our newborns is when they are hungry or fussy. Please hold and nurture your newborn as often as possible because there will be many times, for one reason or another, when you won't be able to.

It is crucial for fathers to feed their daughters, change their diapers, and give them baths. By taking part in these daily activities, fathers are making a statement and commitment to be involved right from the start. More important, everything a father does with his daughter will bring them closer together. One of the things I loved to do was to get down on the carpet at eye level with my daughters and play with them. While playing with your daughter, make sure she has your undivided attention. Don't let television, the phone, or other distractions interrupt your precious time with her. The infant and toddler years are critical periods in children's lives in terms of bonding with their fathers. Years of research has shown that by the time our children are five to six years old they will have developed their character and personality, essentially who they are. Once these years are gone, you will never get them back. So take advantage of the one chance you have as a father with your newborn. Cherish that time, and you will never forget or regret it. The best we can do as fathers is to love our daughters unconditionally, avoid stereotypes, and play an active role in their lives. A newborn is the ideal place to start.

Create a Bond

Much of parenting today is what I call "fast-food parenting." Too many parents are more concerned with the moment or the day rather than taking the time to make decisions and considering the possible long-term effects these decisions might have on their children. It's unlikely that you will ever create a loving bond with your daughter if you take this approach. As parents, many of us think we can just show up to the parenting game already prepared to play. The truth is that many of us have never had training or education in this area. In addition, many of us, including myself, have been without healthy and functional role models while growing up. Most of us probably learned on the fly and continue learning through on-the-job training. How is it that our society holds parenting and family in such high regard, yet many of us spend very little, if any, time trying to be better parents? Sadly, I suspect that many of us are selfish by nature, and if something doesn't come easy for us or doesn't have a dollar sign or a title attached to it, we usually don't spend much time or energy on it.

If you really want to make a difference in

your life and that of your young daughter, take the time to educate yourself on how to be a good parent and a better father. There are countless resources available to us. We need only to seek them out, apply them faithfully, and dedicate ourselves to creating that special bond with our daughters.

CHAPTER 2
Trust and Respect

In any relationship, whether it is personal or professional, the two critical factors for success are mutual trust and respect. These same two factors also play an important part in developing a successful relationship with your daughter.

Building a successful relationship with your daughter will require a combination of hard work, consistency, and follow-through. Not only must you pay close attention to what you say, but how you conduct yourself in the presence of your daughter and family. This means living up to your promises and commitments, setting an example for your daughter, and demonstrating how important these character traits are in a person. When your daughter hears you making promises and commitments that you keep, not only does it build her trust and respect for you, but it also makes her believe she should operate in the same manner. Many of us forget that our daughters have us under constant visual and emotional surveillance. This ongoing surveillance is where they get much of their internal programming that helps build their personal blueprint, including their ability to establish relationships. Therefore, as your daughter witnesses your approach to interacting and communicating with her and others, she is making mental notes. These programmed notes will most likely be used in her formula for developing and maintaining relationships as she grows older.

Other important factors in developing a trusting and respectful relationship are taking a genuine interest in your daughter as a person and being a good listener. As she gets older, get to know her and understand her as a little girl and as a young lady. Sometimes, as parents, we think we know it all and have all the answers. Someone once told me, "God gave us two ears yet only one mouth so we would have a greater capacity for listening rather than talking." Well, many of us should work on becoming better listeners rather than talkers. Listening without an agenda will allow us to improve our chances of having a successful relationship with our daughters.

Please don't make the mistake of waiting too long to develop a relationship based upon respect and trust with your daughter. Stay involved in your daughter's life and try hard to ask lots of meaningful questions. Avoid probing, questions with hidden motives, and being presumptuous. By having an honest, two-way relationship with your daughter, she will feel as if she can consult with you and confide in you about any issue in her life. **Always remember to try and look into the future and imagine what you would like your daughter to think about you.** Would you want her to say, "I didn't see my father much and didn't know him very well, but he always gave me all the money and anything else I wanted"? Would you prefer "My father was always a part of my life, and I will cherish that time and our relationship forever"?

I will never forget when my father passed away several years ago. Because of the poor choices my father made in his life, he had to lie in a hospital bed in his dying days knowing and realizing he had failed as a father, husband, and person. Mentally and physically sick, he died an unhappy person. Tragically, there were no memories for my siblings and me of great times or loving relationships nor were there special moments to reminisce about with him. No, it was all very sad. For me, it was the end to a part of my life that seemed to be a bad dream, which had taken place in another lifetime.

I'm sharing this story with you to emphasize the extreme importance of developing loving, trusting, and respectful relationships in life. I hope you can learn from this and absorb what I've said before: You are the only father your daughter will ever have. If you have the courage to be an active and loving father in your daughter's life, make a commitment today to build the best relationship you know how.

Be Involved

How many times in our lives have we committed to be involved in something and then either lost interest or couldn't find time to follow through? Most of us have been down that road before. I certainly have. However, now we are talking about something very different, our daughters. As fathers, we must get involved in our daughters' lives and stay involved. Once again, this is a case of setting our priorities and deciding what is most important. If we care about how our daughters will view us as fathers, we must stay on track.

Being involved in our daughters' lives requires that we participate on a daily basis. We must know their friends, likes, dislikes, good habits, and not-so-good habits. We must be involved in their schools, their eating habits, sleeping habits, manners, behavior patterns, activities, learning aptitudes, and their abilities to get along with others. If this sounds like a lot of work and a huge commitment, you're right. It most certainly is. Many fathers must change their ways of thinking and break the male/female stereotypes wide open if they plan to succeed as fathers and develop healthy, loving relationships with their daughters.

One tangible way to get involved in your daughter's life is to take a genuine interest in her activities by making yourself present and available. It's one thing to verbally acknowledge the importance of this involvement and tell your daughter you have an interest. However, the most important statement you can make is to be physically and actively involved. Be there. Show up. This includes signing up as a coach, helping on field trips, reading to her class, and teaching her about finances. All of these actions and time spent together demonstrate to her that you really care. It makes her feel as if she's important and emotionally validates her connection with you. I also suggest that fathers make the time to join some sort of father-daughter organization. There are many of these organizations throughout the United States. The best place to research and find one that fits your needs is online. Here are several websites for those of you interested in doing some research: fatheranddaughters.org, fatherhood.org, dads-daughters.com, and fathers.com.

All of this committed involvement sends a clear message to your daughter. The message is that you care, and she is a very important part of your life. Regardless of how busy you profess to be, the less time you spend with your daughter and the less involvement you have in her life will result in a proportionate level of emptiness and a void in both of your lives that can never be completely resolved. Remember, you only have one chance at raising your daughter. Please be involved and stay involved.

Teach with Patience

Sometime after we had our first daughter, my wife and I discussed how critical it was for us to try to be caring teachers, with plenty of patience. This commitment has been difficult at times, and we continually work hard at it. The only way any of us improve at anything is to work hard, and parenting is no exception.

When both of our daughters were first able to talk and communicate with us, we tried to speak to them respectfully, more like adults than toddlers. We spoke in full sentences and explained things to them the best we could. We always tried to avoid one-word responses and answers like, "Because that's the way it is." Those types of feedback don't teach our daughters much at all. Typically, it takes just a few minutes to better explain something or answer their questions. It's easy to say:

"Just because."
"I don't have time."
"Don't ask me now."
"Go ask your mom."
(My personal favorite, but don't tell anyone.)

Sure, most of us are busy, and it's difficult to get into a detailed discussion when we have other commitments. On those occasions when you truly don't have the time to completely answer a question or clarify something to your daughter, gently explain to her why and set a time when you can finish the conversation. It's very important that you stick to that promise and get back to her. *Even if your daughter doesn't remember or has lost interest in that earlier question, you still need to make sure she knows you lived up to your word, and that it was important to you to finish your conversation with her.* None of us are perfect at anything we do in life. Keep that in mind when teaching your daughter and attempting to maintain patience.

A good teacher must be a good listener. Earlier I touched on how crucial being a good listener is. If we expect to teach our daughters about anything, we must develop the ability to interact in a way she recognizes as a two-way street. You accomplish this not only by listening well, but also by asking her plenty of questions and encouraging her to do the same. Once you achieve open and honest dialogue, there's a much better chance that your daughter will confide in you and look to you for advice. Don't have a hidden agenda in your teaching. That's a mistake. Don't be a dictator, bent on having your daughter always see things your way. Be careful; you'll open yourself up to criticism if you don't practice what you preach or profess to know it all.

It's best just to explain to your daughter right up front that you don't have all the answers and never will. Let her know, as a responsible father, you owe it to her to teach her right from wrong and to do the best job you can at preparing her for real-life issues. Remind her that her opinion counts too, and that you always want her to express her opinions and thoughts on any topic. This kind of open dialogue allows your daughter to feel more comfortable with you as an objective teacher. When she feels confident and comfortable, she's more likely to trust and respect what you have to say. Will this be easy all the time? Absolutely not! Like any well-designed plan, you must stick to it, practice plenty of patience, and give it a chance.

A Mind of Her Own

One of the most enjoyable and rewarding experiences I've had is witnessing my daughters make decisions on their own. I'm referring to their healthy, safe, and harmless decisions at three or four years old—decisions like what clothes to wear, what game to play, or what subject to discuss. Letting them make decisions teaches them that they have their own minds.

Sometimes, as fathers, we go a little overboard thinking that our daughters always need us to help them with small tasks and simple day-to-day activities. It's natural for children to start wanting to do things by themselves. The best thing we can do is to help them accomplish these small tasks and activities when they ask. We just have to make sure these activities and tasks are supervised until they do them on their own. At about three years old, both my daughters wanted to start doing many things by themselves, as well as helping my wife and me with certain things. Some of the things included getting their clothes out of their drawers, pouring their milk or water, helping in the yard and around the house, and helping to make cookies. These are normal, healthy requests, and you should take the time to assist your daughters in their new ventures. It would be easy to automatically tell them, "No, you're too young. Just let Daddy do it. I'll let you try it next time." Once again, as fathers, this is just a matter of adjusting our learned behavior and automatic response system. Before you say no, stop for just a few seconds and ask yourself, *Would it really be a problem if I allowed her to do this, or am I just saying no because it's easier?* More often than not, that's the case.

When your daughter asks to do something on her own, try allowing yourself a few seconds before replying. I think you'll be surprised at how many times you might just say, "Sure you can. Give it try, but I'll have to watch you." Often it's too easy to say no. It's better to explain why you say no when you have to. Take a minute to explain to your daughter why she can't do something. No just means no to them, and fathers say it so often that their daughters, who are bright and curious, want to know specifically why they can't do something.

Every time you allow your daughter to do something, the potential end result is that she'll accomplish something and feel good about it. One of the countless things my daughters asked me when they were younger was, "Can I put your belt on for you?"

Well, I could have said to them, "Sorry, Honey. I'm in a hurry, and it's faster for me to do this." However, how much longer did it actually take to let my daughter put the belt on for me? I'll tell you how long, less than a minute. Think about that. It seems to be insignificant, yet it has a tremendous impact on her. First, I'm sending the message that I have time for her. Second, she feels as if she is part of my daily routine. Third, I trusted her to attempt something she asked me to try. Finally, I showed patience and was part of her success in an activity. Now how big do you think that insignificant request is? This kind of interaction and activity builds your daughter's confidence and self-esteem and can make a huge difference in her ability to use her own mind and feel involved in the decision-making process. Ask yourself if you'd rather your daughter be able to make her own decisions as she gets older or be constantly relying on someone else?

No One is Perfect

How often do you find yourself getting upset with your daughter because she's angry about something, raises her voice, or disagrees with you? If you're anything like the rest of us, it happens quite often. Try to remember, just like you and me, our daughters have good and bad days, and they are not perfect. In addition, they will also act out in many ways as part of their maturing process, while exploring their boundaries.

I can tell you from personal experience, if you take the time to research and understand child development and the challenges children face, you'd learn to have more patience. A natural part of your daughter's personality and character development is the need to dispute, challenge, and test you as a father to establish healthy boundaries and to distinguish right from wrong and good from bad. Think about it. How in the world would a three-year-old girl know right from wrong or anything about boundaries? She wouldn't, and that's why, as fathers, we need to better understand our daughters' actions and behavior in order to raise them in a healthy, productive environment. Thousands of child development books and articles are readily available. I strongly encourage all fathers to make good use of them. These resources will make fathering your daughter a lot easier and will enhance your chances of developing a healthy, loving relationship with your daughter.

In addition, what about your daughter having good days, bad days, and maybe not feeling so well? Make sure you keep an eye on this and have the patience to understand that this stuff happens. Why is it acceptable or normal for older children and adults to be in bad moods or have bad days, but because younger children can't yet articulate their feelings adequately, many of us assume they are misbehaving, being disrespectful, or being brats? Does that make any sense, and do you think it's fair? I certainly don't, so please work hard and consider these issues when dealing with your young daughter. Many times when she gets upset, tells you no, or acts out in any number of ways, it could just be part of her maturing, understanding right from wrong, or establishing boundaries. The best way to handle this is with caring patience.

Maybe you think I'm living in a fantasy world and don't know how hard it is to deal with an angry, disobedient child. Well, certainly parenting is difficult at times, and each of has our own unique challenges. However, we have a responsibility as fathers to be the leaders in our families and role models for how to handle these conflicts and negative situations. If we lose control, yell, scream, or even hit our young daughters for misbehaving, what are we really teaching them? To act like us when they get mad? There's a good chance they'll grow up and handle their anger the same way we do. Do you want that?

The point I'm trying to make here is that you need to respond in a caring way to your daughter's anger and disrespectful comments instead of overreacting. For example, if she yells, try to lower your voice during the altercation. If she starts being disrespectful or saying mean things and refuses to listen, tell her you will not listen to her until she can talk to you in an appropriate manner. It is up to you as a father to set the standard for how conflict and confrontation are handled. Therefore, if you feel the situation is getting out of control or you're losing your temper, take a timeout or allow her one until things cool down. Even though it's tough to avoid, don't engage in a shouting match with your young daughter. You're the role model and adult. Sometimes when all else fails, try giving her a big hug. When we get angry, the best thing to do is to back off, cool down, and agree to talk later. Believe me, I was raised in a household where both parents were always yelling and shouting at each other and at us kids. To this day, I must constantly work to stifle this learned behavior and not to raise my voice when I get upset. I promised my wife and daughters I would continue to work on this.

Always try to communicate calmly rather than raise your voice and automatically discipline. More often than not, your young daughter's outbursts, frustrations, anger, and antagonism are related to developmental issues, bad moods, bad days, or like us, they're just not perfect.

Let Her Teach You

One of the most natural things for us to do as fathers is to teach our daughters. That's great as long as we realize we can also learn from them. They have such a unique perspective of life and often see things we don't because of our busy, complicated lives.

Every time I get a chance, I watch and listen to my daughters play by themselves, with each other, or with friends. If you haven't taken the time to do this yet, you owe it to yourself to try. My girls have come up with some of the best stories, games, and other activities, and they always add their own twists to them. If we allow our daughters to explore, venture out, and be spontaneous, they'll continue to develop strong personal skills that will help them immensely as they get older. All of these activities at home, at school, or with their friends afford them the opportunity to start learning and storing valuable information. They will start to use this knowledge in all areas of their lives and apply it to day-to-day decisions and interactions with others. Between the ages of three to five, girls begin to develop their own personalities and philosophies. Once they enter this phase, we can start learning from them.

Start asking your daughter plenty of questions about day-to-day activities like playing, learning, and reading. Encourage her to ask you lots of questions too. This type of interaction and verbal exchange will create a tighter bond, encouraging her to learn from you and vice versa. If we watch carefully, we'll see our daughters express emotions, and for the most part, they'll speak openly and honestly about almost anything. It can be embarrassing, because often they point out our flaws and shortcomings at the most inopportune times. Occasionally, in front of other people, my daughters ask, "Daddy, how come your hair is gray? Does that mean you're old?" Or "Daddy, how come you have lines next to your eyes?" These types of questions are normal and painfully honest. Most children desire to learn, and one of the best ways is to ask questions. Fathers tend to feel they must always be there to answer their daughters' questions, yet have a difficult time asking them questions. Every chance you get, ask your daughter about her activities, her school, her friends, her meals, and her favorite music. This accomplishes at least two things. First, it makes your daughter feel important because you care enough to hear her answers. Second, the more you know about your daughter the better your chances are to create that special trusting and open relationship.

Also important, encourage your daughter to speak openly and honestly with you even if it means that she's critical of you at times. I had an eye-opening experience when my oldest daughter, Rachel, was seven years old. I was coaching her softball team, my first experience at coaching a girls' team. It was also Rachel's first year playing an organized sport. So when the first game arrived, it was a little nerve-racking for both of us. She was playing center field, and at that age level, coaches are allowed to roam the field while their teams are on defense. A ball was hit to her, and she just watched it go by her. I said, "Rachel, what are you doing? You have to get the ball." She looked at me a little frustrated and then ran after the ball. A few plays later, another ball was hit to her. Again, she watched it go right by. I again said, "Rachel, I told you, you can't just stand there; you have to try and stop the ball."

She became a little more upset, looked right at me and said, "Dad, what do you expect?

It's only my first game." Well, I felt really bad at that moment. She was absolutely right; it was her first game. Even though we'd practiced prior to the season, she was still learning. I immediately apologized to Rachel, told her she was right, and told her that I never should have expected so much from her at this stage of the season. After the game, I apologized again and explained to her I wanted so badly for her to do well that I'd over-reacted and lost sight of the fact that the season had just started.

Later that evening, something else occurred to me about that softball game and Rachel's reaction to my comments that made me feel very good. I realized that she was secure enough in our relationship to tell me exactly the way she felt instead of trying to make me feel better or to please me. In other words, she could have said, "Sorry, Dad. I'll try and do better next time." The fact is that she didn't, and that made me happy. I will always remember moments like that because they reinforce the importance of a healthy, open relationship between us.

The final point I want to make about that same softball game concerns allowing our daughters to teach us. I, too, could have reacted differently when Rachel spoke back to me. I could have replied, "That's no excuse; you should know better. Rachel, don't argue with me. Just go get the ball." However, I didn't react that way because I respect her and can learn from her. That's right. I learned something from my seven-year-old daughter. Her willingness to respond to me with confidence and security and my willingness to listen and respect what she had to say taught me to be more accepting and patient. I had to calm down and realize that the season was young; Rachel would have many other chances and gradually improve. If she and I hadn't worked on our relationship the previous seven years, we most likely would have had a different exchange during that game.

Make sure you admit when you're wrong and apologize. During Rachel's softball game, I overreacted, so I apologized. As fathers, we often find it difficult to admit we were wrong. We're not perfect either. We make mistakes like everyone else, but we need to lead by example. It's important for your daughter to learn for herself the appropriate time to admit when she is wrong about something and apologize. She has you under surveillance and will follow your lead more than you might realize. Let your daughter teach you about herself—and about yourself.

CHAPTER 3
School and Education

Somewhere along the way, many parents have come to the conclusion that the school system and teachers should be responsible for raising their children. Possibly, it's because children are in school most of the day, or they come home and say things or do things that parents haven't seen or heard before. It could be that if our children don't have good grades or good study habits we think the system is failing. There are any number of reasons this could be occurring, and some of them are valid no doubt. Nevertheless, we should clearly distinguish and understand the difference between what we should be doing for our children and what the school system should be doing.

The school system and teachers are there to educate our daughters and to prepare them for their lives from a professional, occupational, and intellectual standpoint. The school systems are not designed to raise our daughters, to teach them right from wrong, or to be a good person and responsible citizen. This is a job for parents. Don't misunderstand me; I realize that teachers have a responsibility to address certain issues with our daughters in class and to identify and report them if necessary to administrators and parents. However, characteristically what our daughters bring to school was learned at home. Because of this, parents must take a more active and responsible role in their daughters' lives.

Make sure you get involved and stay involved with your daughter's school activities and the educational process. This includes attending parent/teacher meetings, asking questions, and getting to know your daughter's teachers. This also includes helping out with homework, attending school functions, and volunteering for projects and activities that will allow you to play an active role. By being involved, you can better identify issues that might come up, whether good or bad. You will have a better chance of becoming familiar with the school's curriculum and surroundings. You'll also send a clear message to your daughter and to the school she attends that you care enough to be involved and support the system. As fathers, we don't have the right to complain about our school system and teachers unless we are actively involved in the process, voicing our opinions and concerns.

I also recommend that fathers keep an eye on the school curriculum, the playground, and break-time activities. Occasionally, ask to sit in on a few of your daughter's classes and observe the way the teacher conducts his or her class. Make sure the school treats both boys and girls equally. Be sure that physical and sporting activities are not unbalanced or gender biased.

Please make sure, regardless of your background, you promote and advocate the importance of education. Don't make the mistake of intentionally or covertly passing your past educational experiences and beliefs onto your daughter. Provide her with facts about education and educated people and explain to her that what she learns in life can never be taken away by anyone. Reams of statistics tell us that those who go on to get a college education have a much better chance of succeeding at anything they attempt in life. My last plea is that we, as fathers, stay away from societal prejudices and stereotypes that suggest when girls grow up that they should "just hope to find a man to take care of them." This is one of the most uninformed statements one can utter, and yet it still exists because of narrow-minded people in every society. The way to avoid this type of mentality is, once again, to work hard to help fight stereotypes, for your daughter's sake. Make your daughter's education a priority, and keep in mind that as she gets older, her education is an integral part of her independence, personal philosophy, level of confidence, and self-esteem.

What a formal education won't teach her . . .

A formal education and an advanced degree are among the most important achievements and accomplishments in one's life and pave the way for additional opportunity and income-earning ability. There are many well-documented statistics regarding the value of a formal education. However, one of the most compelling is that those who don't go on to graduate with a four-year degree of any kind have more than a 50% chance of making $25,000 a year or less. That figure is near the poverty level if you have four or more children. However, equally critical to success are the many other lessons in life that should be taught, lived, and experienced—which a formal education is unable to teach your young daughter. These are the areas fathers need help exploring if they want to provide their girls with the best opportunities available.

One frustration I still have with the formal education process is that it's driven primarily by grades and for the most part hasn't changed much over the past several decades. Don't get me wrong; I realize there has to be some kind of grading system. I'm frustrated by the way most schools administer grades, because they create an environment where young children think there's something wrong with them if they don't get A's or B's. Some kids spend hours studying a particular subject, working on it as hard as they can, but still don't score well on tests and end up getting poor grades in those courses. Yet the same young children may put the same amount of energy and effort into entirely different subjects, score well on the tests, and end up with excellent grades.

Common sense would have most of us asking, "Why does this happen?" It's very simple really; every single one of us, no matter what age, is just naturally better at some things than others. Does that make someone less of a person or less likely to succeed in life? Of course not, but this is how most formal education systems are designed to teach us and to make us feel.

How do we change the perception of this system and avoid this segregating-type activity by subject matter? The only way to change is for teachers, administrators, and parents to talk to their young children and explain that grades are important, but they are not everything. Tell your young daughter that as long as she studies hard and does the best she can to learn a subject, the grade and the rest will take care of itself. Meaning, she is no less of a person because she did the best she could yet still received a C, while others in her class received A's and B's. We must be careful when discussing this information with our daughters so that they clearly understand the difference between slacking off and doing the very best they can. That way they don't misunderstand our intentions and use this as an excuse to not work hard and apply themselves.

Educational systems, like other systems and organizations out there in the world, have somehow adopted this segregation mentality that tends to promote and breed egos based purely on the grades or the titles one gets. We need to discuss these realities with our young daughters so they have a better understanding of what they are up against and what they should watch out for as they get older and enter the work place.

There are many areas we should focus on as fathers with our young daughters that a formal education doesn't teach them. Most of them are addressed in this book. They have labels like "Ways, Hows, and Whys." The way we parent. The way we treat people. The way we conduct our lives. The way we lead by example. The way we approach adversity, and the way we act toward other people. How we spend our time. How we plan for the future. How we have fun. How we show our emotions. How we show our love. How we respect each other and how we listen. Why we never stop learning. Why we eat properly. Why we exercise regularly. Why we always work hard. Why we never give up. Why we always learn to forgive. Why we love one another, and why we always pray.

As much as we need a formal education and should continue promoting it as a priority in our young daughters' lives, please make sure your daughter understands these institutions and how they operate. Just as important, teach her all the things that a formal education won't teach her.

CHAPTER 4
Eating Habits and Body Image

As fathers, we must do a better job at promoting and advocating physical exercise and well-balanced and healthy eating habits for our daughters. Our society currently has a very serious problem with overweight, unhealthy, and inactive adults and children. We are the richest and most resourceful nation and spend the most money on diet and exercise-related products, yet we continue gaining more weight and becoming less active. One reason for this is that many people are looking everywhere else for the magic solution and quick fix instead of taking personal responsibility for making a lifestyle change and sticking with it. We owe it to ourselves and certainly to our young daughters to create an environment that promotes healthy, active lifestyles.

As with other important areas of our daughters' lives, we must take charge and be involved with their eating habits and exercise. We must also practice what we preach. Meaning, we can't expect our daughters to respect us and follow our lead when we live a double standard in what we say and what we do. How can we tell them sodas are not good for us if we can drink them just because we're adults? How much sense does that make? By the same token, why would you allow your daughter to eat fast food on a regular basis, yet not eat it yourself because you think it's unhealthy? Does that make sense?

The value of nutrition has taken a back seat and become a low priority for many parents. They have adopted a lifestyle that promotes the adage, "I don't have time." *I don't have time to eat right. I don't have time to exercise. I don't have time for my spouse. I don't have time for my children. I don't have time to read. I don't have time to take a vacation. I don't have time to enjoy life.* What do we have time for, and where are we spending our time? We must make time for the things in our lives that are important and more meaningful. We must stop thinking selfishly for the moment and look to the future. What we allow our daughters to put in their bodies today and the way we approach our own eating habits will have a lasting effect on them as adults.

As soon as your daughter begins eating solid foods, have a strategy in place to promote healthy eating habits. Consult with your pediatrician about what your daughter should be eating and what foods are best for her. Make a list of questions for her pediatrician before each visit so you can take advantage of your daughter's checkups. Include questions about the types of foods you should be serving her and disciplines regarding meal times. My wife and I are fortunate to have a wonderful pediatrician. She's always inquired about the food we serve our daughters and advised us to make sure we are the ones in charge of food choices and meal times.

Too often children dictate what they want to eat and when, instead of the parents. Parents must also lead by example. In our house, we've never outlawed junk food and nonnutritive items; we simply regulate the amount consumed. Nonnutritive food and soft drinks are considered once-in-a-while food and drinks. We let our girls pick any cereal they wish when we go on vacation or for a few weeks during summer vacation or holidays. Occasionally, we allow each one to choose a place to eat out. Otherwise, we focus mainly on preparing healthy and nutritional meals and eating at home. We try very hard to eat dinner together as a family every evening. I'm a big fan of moderation and balance with just about everything in life. In moderation, most food and beverage is not going to cause long-term, negative effects.

Many of us neglect the important role nutrition plays in our daughters' education, their learning abilities, and their energy levels. If they don't get the appropriate meals and nutrition, we risk the chance of sending them to school with a learning disadvantage. Their minds and bodies need and require real nutrition to achieve maximum comprehension and learning. For example: We can't expect maximum results from our daughters when we start them off in the morning with a sugared cereal, followed by an artificially-processed lunch—filled with preservatives, high levels of sugar, salt, and other garbage.

Spend some time reading nutritional books and educating yourself about the benefits of eating well and the cautions for eating otherwise. Make sure you talk to your daughter about nutrition and revisit the subject often. Take the time to explain to her the reasons for the different types of foods and why some are healthier than others. Educating your young daughter at home about nutrition will reinforce her chances of maintaining good eating habits now and as she gets older. Be sure you develop and adhere to healthy eating habits as well. If not, you will undermine your credibility with your daughter.

Notice that up to this point I haven't used the words diet or focused on the words *fat, thin,* or *skinny?* My wife and I have always agreed that we would try very hard not to use these words around our daughters. I dislike what the word diet has come to imply, something temporary. If people want to lose weight, get in better shape, or improve the way they feel physically, they should make permanent lifestyle changes. I know there are always exceptions, and some people have real emotional and physical challenges that plague them. However, most diets set people up for the quick fix, followed by long-term failure, unlike a true lifestyle change that is permanent. Around our house, we use words like healthy or unhealthy versus skinny and fat. We also explained to our daughters how all people are different, and that's what makes this world so wonderful.

Society in general and most forms of media perpetrate an image of the ideal girl or woman. The problem is that this is an unrealistic and potentially dangerous image. The end result is that females of all ages feel as if they must resemble these advertisers' ideals in order to be accepted or beautiful.

Here are some statistics regarding body image: Overall, 90% of all girls, aged three to eleven, have at least one Barbie® doll each, an early role model with a figure that is essentially unattainable in real life. At age thirteen, 53% of American girls are "unhappy with their bodies." This figure reaches 78% by the time girls reach seventeen. In addition, 80% of ten-year-old American girls diet. The number one wish for young girls, aged eleven to seventeen, is to be thinner. [1]

These poor girls and women feel that by altering their appearances and bodies they'll be accepted by society and command the attention of boys and men. This couldn't be further from the truth. This image issue has become a serious problem, causing millions of female health problems and eating disorders. We fathers need to accept that many young girls have health issues and confused identities because they never really had a healthy, loving relationship with their fathers or positive male figures in their lives. Our daughters need to know and feel that they are adored regardless of their looks and body types. As a father, if you don't step in and get involved with your daughter's life and understand what she might be going through, she will suffer. We need to reassure our daughters of how much we love them, just the way they are. We need to instill in them the notion that a decent, respectable person is more than an image and a body. A good and caring person is made from the inside out and not the outside in.

Sports, Exercise, and Physical Activities

Not too many years ago, we wouldn't even be discussing or writing about how important sports and other physical activities are to girls and women. However, with the recent popularity and explosion of female sports, many parents are realizing the residual benefits of their daughters being involved in one or more sports or activities.

Traditionally, organized sports were associated with young boys growing up and with men. While there's absolutely nothing wrong with that rich tradition, there's definitely something wrong with this historical stereotype and its effect on our daughters. In the past ten years or so, sports and activities for females have been recognized and validated, not only by the majority of people but by educational institutions and by the media. Although female sports have come a long way, there remains a lingering gender prejudice and hidden level of resistance by many people and organizations. This resistance typically stems from schools or organizations that don't want to share or take away funds from male sports programs. Other possible reasons include the desire to suppress the athletic and competitive experience for girls and women or to impede them from acquiring greater self-confidence and a sense of achievement from these activities. God forbid that this type of personal fulfillment ultimately could lead to a time when girls and women would start looking for something other than boys and men to satisfy their every interest and need.

Please forgive my obvious sarcasm, but the truly scary thing is that what I've said above is true. However, getting people or organizations to admit to this line of thinking would prove them politically incorrect or ignorant of current popular opinion. Their reasoning is disguised or spun in a way that sounds legitimate or politically accept-able.

The good news is that things have improved and will continue to improve if we fathers stay involved. Today there are many wonderful advance-ments in female sports and activities. We need to piggyback on these successes and continue to sup-port, first and foremost, our local sports programs for girls and women at all levels. It starts when your daughter is very young. It could be softball, basketball, tennis, swimming, golf, dance, soccer, or whatever. Regardless of the sport or activity, make sure you're involved, and let your daughter know you support her and her efforts.

Make yourself available to the coaches or program leaders; consider coaching at some level or getting involved as an assistant or substitute. By getting involved and taking an interest in your daughter's activity, you send a clear message to her that you not only care about what she's doing, but you also care enough to be involved and participate yourself. Recent research from the dads-daugh-ters.com website shows that women who are suc-cessful in sports usually have involved fathers who encourage and support their pursuits.

Over and above the traditional sports and formal activities offered to our daughters, don't forget the importance of exercising on a regular basis. Too often, many of us fathers focus so much on the activity itself that we forget about the phys-ical conditioning required. To properly prepare for these activities, your daughter must maintain a level of conditioning and endurance that will allow her to compete safely and remain healthy.

I've coached girls' softball and boys' baseball for the past few years, and I can tell you the majority of the children playing sports today are unhealthy and completely out of shape. It's sad when you ask a group of eight- or nine-year-old boys or girls to jog, not run, to the end of the field and back, and over half are out of breath. A few can't make it back without stopping to rest. This is the result of children not getting enough physical exercise and not eating a well-balanced diet.

Another leading contributor to the lack of physical activity and exercise is the sedentary activities our daughters enjoy these days, such as video and computer games, television, and surfing the Internet. These indoor activities have become convenient babysitters for many parents and a way of life for our daughters at a very young age. Let's examine the average daily routine for many elementary and grade school children. First, they spend six to seven hours sitting in classrooms during school, where in many cases there is little if any physical education and sports activity. Second, they get out of school, and if they aren't participating in after-school sports or other physical activities, they probably go home or hang out with friends. Third, at home these days, the most popular activities are the sedentary ones mentioned above. Fourth, after dinner, and ideally homework, many kids go back to television, etc. Last but not least, hopefully, they go to bed at a decent time and sleep for eight to ten hours.

Now what's wrong with the picture I just painted? Over the course of each day, how much physical activity does the average grade school child get? Almost none. Couple that fact with the very good chance that most of those kids aren't eating well, and you have a formula for an epidemic of unhealthy, unfit children. This epidemic is real and should be taken seriously. Please don't think these are my opinions and personal beliefs alone. Do your own research, and you'll uncover the alarming statistics about the staggering number of children who are obese or have diabetes. Simply put, many of our children are out of shape and eating their way to devastating health problems that could appear as soon as their early twenties.

You should take this information seriously and make sure you pay attention to your daughter's eating habits and exercise pattern. As soon as your baby girl learns to walk, make physical activities and daily exercise a priority in her life. Take walks every day, starting with her in a stroller. When she begins to walk on her own, slowly make outdoor walking and other activities an ongoing routine. As she gets older, introduce bike riding, skating, hiking, etc. Once she's five or six years old, introduce sports and other physical activities such as softball, golf, soccer, dance, ballet, and swimming.

As your daughter matures, see if she takes a stronger interest in a particular sport or activity. If so, talk to her about her interests to see if she wants to narrow her focus and energy to one or two sports or activities. No matter what she chooses, continue to promote and encourage her to play as long as she can or is willing to. Statistics show that young girls who continue to play sports or are involved in an organized activity through high school and college are 70% to 80% less likely to become pregnant at an early age or regularly use drugs and alcohol. Do yourself and your daughter a big favor; make sports and activities a part of your lives.

Religion and Spirituality

What in the world would human beings do without religion or their religious beliefs? Don't get me wrong; it's wonderful that people are passionate about their beliefs. Healthy, functional passion is one of the greatest gifts we could ask for. However, have you ever wondered why so many people dislike others simply because of their different religious beliefs? If you believe in God, do you think God ever intended for all of us to look alike, act alike, and have the same beliefs? If this seems confusing, imagine what our young daughters are up against every day.

I started the chapter this way purposely for two different reasons. First, think about what beliefs, if any, you have about God, a religion, and spirituality. Second, try to explore the reasoning behind your beliefs or disbeliefs and how one or the other could affect your young daughter and your relationship with her. You might be asking yourself, "What is this guy talking about and what does this have to do with father and daughter relationships?" Let me try my best to explain.

All religions get a bad rap at one time or another from those who are unable to understand what a real, God-loving, spiritual person is about. Truly religious people are able to love and accept others unconditionally, without prejudice or self-serving motives. For the most part, those people who criticize aren't actually against religion. They may have their own ideas and beliefs and simply stereotype others because of their choices of religion. Maybe they haven't taken the time to educate themselves on the true meaning of healthy religion and spiritually.

One of my favorite statements about religion and spirituality came from Dr. Wayne Dyer. He's often said, "Religion divides, while spirituality unites." It is a very powerful and accurate statement. Unfortunately, many times when we attach a physical label, title, or category to someone or something, we start the process of division. When we start dividing, we create egos, arrogance, segregation, power struggles, and stereotypes. Somewhere along the way, many of us have lost sight of religion's true meaning and purpose—to worship God, to serve mankind, to be kind to people, to love unconditionally, and to treat others equally regardless of their nationality, race, gender, or religious beliefs.

Please make note of the examples I've just described because these are the types of comments and people to which your daughter will be exposed. Depending upon the approach you take in introducing the subject to your daughter, you will impact her early decisions regarding religion and spirituality.

I am a strong advocate of spirituality and a believer in God. However, this strong conviction didn't come to me naturally while growing up. It wasn't until later in life that I fully understood how religion and spirituality could so positively change my life. I was raised a Catholic and never really understood why or for what reason. This, again, was a case of learned behavior during my childhood and being a product of my environment. The fault almost never lies with the religion to which you were exposed, as much as with the type of environment or people to whom you were exposed and grew up around.

Here's the point. Make absolutely sure that you develop a clear, healthy, and unbiased approach to religion and spirituality when introducing it to your young daughter. Make certain you clean your religious slate of all past experiences, heartaches, anger, dysfunction, and stereotypes before potentially passing them on to her. Otherwise, you risk repeating some of the same mistakes many of our grandparents and parents in previous generations committed regarding religion. Whether you're a religious person or not, you owe it to your young daughter to objectively discuss the options with her and help educate her about religion and spirituality. It may or may not become an important part of her life, but are you willing to make that decision for her or allow her to make her own decision without healthy and caring guidance?

Personally, I want my young daughters to know there is a great Creator in God, and that every day when we wake up, take a breath, take a step, and speak a word, we should thank God. I also want them to know that they are made in the very image of God, and a living part of their spirits can learn to trust in God and be accountable to Him. As a family, we pray with our daughters, and they pray on their own as well. Oftentimes, it's more difficult for men and fathers to pray with their daughters or in front of them. I had my own challenges with this early on. However, it is so important for fathers to make praying with their daughters a priority and a regular practice. Praying together will strengthen the spiritual and emotional bond between father and daughter. This spiritual and emotional bond is critical, because it's not physical. It's an emotional connection between father and daughter, which is often times, the most difficult for fathers to achieve with their daughters. If fathers can develop both the physical and emotional connection with their young daughters, the chance for a successful and loving relationship will be greater.

Our nation's young children are in desperate need of love and structure, and apparently, many parents are just too busy to handle this daunting task. If this is the case, to whom will these children turn to in times of need and despair? Other than their parents, whom can they look to and trust? What if their parents don't care? Our children need guidance and direction, and they need to know they can count on someone other than their parents. If you're not already a healthy, objective religious or spiritual person, I encourage you to explore the possibilities for yourself and your daughter. If you happen to be exploring or thinking about this subject, here are two of my favorite writers and best-selling authors. Dr. Wayne W. Dyer: *There Is a Spiritual Solution to*

Every Problem. I also highly recommend the work of Dr. Charles Stanley, one of the most incredible and inspirational leaders of the Christian faith. He delivers a powerful and remarkable message and has published countless books, CDs, and tapes.

CHAPTER 5
"Daddy, play with us."

The contents of this chapter are very special to me and responsible in part for my inspiration to write this book. For such a short, simple expression, "Daddy, play with us," is a tremendously powerful statement. Powerful, because early on your young daughter is asking you to spend time with her the only way she knows how. It seems so natural, yet many men still don't understand the true meaning behind playtime and its powerful impact.

From the first days of both my daughters' lives, continuing through the present, I have always made playtime important. Ever since my daughters could speak well enough, I can remember on a daily basis that both of my daughters would make the request, "Daddy, play with us." This daily request started to diminish at about age seven or eight, but even now, they still ask once in a while. When my daughters were younger, one of the first things they wanted to do when they first saw me was to play with me. Together, my daughters and I have made up at least ten of our own games and have named them as well. The names and brief descriptions of these games are listed in the next section of this chapter. These newly created games and their names are unique, and my wife suggested many times that I write them down and make them part of a book someday. Well, here I am, doing just that and enjoying it very much.

As I mentioned in previous chapters, being involved in your daughter's life and playing an active role as a father is vital. If there were ever a simple place to start a connection with your daughter, it would be just to play with her. Don't misunderstand me; simply playing with her and doing nothing else doesn't qualify you as a fully participating father. Yet it is one of the most important pieces of the father/daughter relationship puzzle. The reason for this is that your daughter's request for you to play with her comes naturally and helps create one of the earliest bonds there is between you. Each time you play together, whether it's making funny faces at her, rolling a ball back and forth, or chasing her through the hallway, all of these interactions validate her importance in your life and bring the two of you closer. It also allows your daughter to make a connection with you and to identify with something you both enjoy. While you're having fun, your daughter feels good because she is a part of it. This is exactly why it is so important to become involved with other areas of your daughter's life. Anytime she feels she has a connection and can identify with you as a father, she will have a better chance to increase her confidence level and excel in other ways, as she grows older.

One mistake many fathers make is that they continue to repeat gender stereotypes when introducing their daughters to playtime events and activities. My hope is that fathers work very hard at offering a diverse menu of activities that includes not only dolls and building blocks but also dress-up and sports. The only way we can achieve this is to be mindful of our mission as participating fathers and to be a part of our daughters' playtime activities. Now run off and play for a while!

Games We Play . . .

As I mentioned earlier, a part of my inspiration for writing this book came from the fun games my daughters and I created over the years. Now, sitting here, actually writing this chapter, I find myself smiling right away, thinking back about the great moments I had and still have with my daughters. There was something very special about these games because they were thought out, designed, and originally only played by my daughters and me. So let's play!

• **Roller Monster**–I'd lie completely stretched out on the living room carpet and roll my entire body back and forth trying to get the girls. As I got closer to them, the object of the game was for them to try and continually jump over me without touching the Roller Monster (me) as I rolled back and forth. We repeated this back and forth activity over and over again.

• **Don't Cross the Bridge**–I'd lie on my stomach completely stretched out on the carpet in a stationary position. The object of the game was for the girls to Cross Over the Bridge (me) to the other side, by stepping on my back without falling. As they stepped on my back, I'd move my body back and forth, like a wobbly bridge trying to make them lose their balance and fall.

• **Blind Chick-A-Dee**–I'd blindfold myself in a certain area of the house and count to five, and then stumble about trying to locate the girls. The object was to try and sense where the girls were by listening to them moving around the room and for me to try and find them and tag them.

• **Surfing USA**–I'd lay a blanket down on the carpet and have one girl at a time stand up on the other end. Then I pulled the blanket around while she stood on the blanket, similar to a surfer on a surfboard riding a wave. The object was for me to pull her around the entire living room, through the dining room and the kitchen, and back to the living room without her falling off the blanket.

• **Roofball**–I'd throw a baseball or softball onto the roof as high as I could, to the peak of the house. The girls would be standing back a distance from the eaves when I did this. The object was for them to come running up and time their approach so that they could catch the ball as it came flying from the roof.

•**Daddy Doll**–I'd lie on the carpet and pretend I was a giant doll. The object was for the girls to try and pull me up, move me around, pull on my arms and legs, and prop me up like a doll. They would move me around in as many different positions as they could.

• **Daddy's Hairdo**–I'd sit in a chair or on the couch while the girls took turns trying different hairdos on me, even using hair clips.

• **Sit and Drop**–I'd lie on the carpet completely stretched out on one side, and the girls would sit on my other side. Then I'd shift my weight extremely fast one direction or the other, and the object was for the girls to drop to either side.

• **Stuffed Little Girls**–I'd take pillows and clothing and stuff the girls' pajamas, tops and bottoms, so they looked like round, plump snowwomen. They were very little at the time, and after stuffing their clothes extremely full, they'd start wrestling. When they fell down, it was almost impossible for them to get back up. This was by far one of the funniest things we ever did!

• **Upside Down Table Pull**–I'd turn a small, plastic table upside down so that one of the girls fit snugly in the center, all four legs pointing up around her. Then I'd tie a rope to one of the table legs and pull her around the lawn in circles and back and forth. Upside down, the table made the perfect sled, which could be quickly drawn across the lawn while she struggled to stay balanced on board.

• **Garbage Dump**–When the girls were between two and five years old, they would stand at an imaginary curb with their arms stretched out wide, and I would play a garbage truck. I'd make a noise like a truck, come up behind one of them, slide my arms beneath her arms, forklift her high in the air, and take her for a ride around the house before disposing of the garbage by dumping her on her back onto the couch.

• **Catch the bus**–This one got a little dangerous at times, but it was fun. One girl at a time would stand up on the couch, and I'd come by the couch fairly quickly. The object was for her to leap from the couch onto my back as I passed by on the move. So it was all about timing as she leapt onto me as I quickly moved by the couch, like a bus picking her up and taking her to her final destination, which was either the bedroom to sleep or the bathroom to brush her teeth.

• **Standing Long Jump**–The girls would stand up on our bed, and one at a time, each would try to jump as far as she could into my arms. The object was to see how far they could jump in midair from the bed to my arms. They would start by jumping just a few feet away into my arms, and after each successful jump, we'd increase the distance until they jumped as far as they could.

I will cherish these moments forever. They are some of the funniest times we've ever had. I never laughed so hard. Those of you who've done similar things with your kids, I'm certain you can relate to the feeling you get by creating something so special with them. For me and for my daughters as well, this was so much fun, partly because there was no structure, no rules, no limitations, and no people telling us what to do and how to do it.

As fathers, we have a tendency to want

some kind of structure, a plan in place, or a strategy behind things, even when it's playtime. Although we mean well, we should try to be more open-minded and creative, ask our daughters from time to time what it is they want to do, and let it happen. You'll be surprised at what they come up with. Fathers should try to encourage their creativity and invent activities for a couple of good reasons: First, to lead by example and show your daughter it's okay for both you and her to have fun, to be creative, and to be carefree. Second, this type of unstructured activity will help establish one of the most enjoyable and special bonds you could imagine with your young daughter. From a little girl's perspective, these types of games will be even more meaningful and important to her if her father is conducting them without gender bias. So make sure they aren't geared towards traditional or stereotypical female activities.

Cooking, Baking, Cleaning, and Laundry

You've already read a lot in this book about my frustrations with gender stereotypes. Here we are in the 21st century, and we still have many men, women, and children who think there are some jobs and chores that are appropriate only for men and others only for women. Does this amaze you as much as it does me, or am I being too sensitive? I realize this issue has improved a great deal over the years, but if you listen to and observe your family and friends closely, you might be surprised at how many gender stereotypes still exist.

Actually, this is one of the few areas that turned out to be a positive for me while growing up in my family. The reason being, my siblings and I had no choice (at a very young age) but to learn how to cook and clean for ourselves, as well as perform other chores. In addition, our grandparents and parents cooked and baked when we were young. Since we had to do most of the household chores and watched our parents doing them as well, they just came more naturally to us, as we grew older.

Still, I had friends in college and roommates who were lost in the kitchen unless it had something to do with the barbeque. I also had friends who had to take their laundry to their mothers' houses every week in order to have clean clothes to wear. Here again is another case of learned behavior and a form of conditioning most of us experienced while growing up. As we become adults, we naturally mimic these habits unless we recognize the problems they cause and make adjustments.

As fathers, we should be working hard to break through these stereotypes and demonstrate to our young daughters that it's normal for us to make dinner, bake cookies from scratch, or do the laundry. It's also normal for mothers to mow the lawn, wash the car, or handle the family's bills and investments. Note that this exercise of helping each other out, of fathers and mothers learning to experience new roles otherwise foreign to them, is not necessarily so that we become an expert in any one of these areas. The purpose is to demonstrate to our young daughters that there is no such thing as a job, chore, or activity that is meant specifically for a man or a woman.

I have baked with my daughters since they were about two years old. My daughters have a number of different items they refer to as "*Daddy's.*" The peanut butter and chocolate cookies we've made together many times are referred to as Daddy's cookies. Because I have made these cookies with them many times since they were young, they once asked my wife if she knows how to make cookies. (I find this hysterical, but my wife doesn't always agree.) When fathers attempt to make cooking and baking fun, our young daughters find that these activities become more enjoyable, rather than boring chores or work. Try to initiate fun rituals with your daughters surrounding these activities so they become positive. My daughters and I have a Saturday and Sunday morning ritual of making hot chocolate, cinnamon toast, or pancake cutouts. The great thing about these long-time rituals is that they are at an age now where they still get excited about doing these activities together, but they now do most of the work themselves and just want me involved and part of the activity. We also do yard work, clean up the house, and do laundry together. We don't do these activities and chores every day, and we do some more than others. However, we do them and have done them together often enough that it makes a huge difference for my daughters, my wife, and me.

I encourage fathers to join in and work at breaking these stereotypes regarding household chores and activities. Take a look at the daily household activities and chores, and if you're not already participating in some or all of them, get going! Start with just one or two, and work your way up to more of them as you go. Talk to your girls about these activities and chores and explain to them that the entire family should be involved, not just either a mother or father. You'll have more success if you make this a positive and fun experience for you and your daughters.

CHAPTER 6
Same-Page Parenting

So far, I have covered many areas that will help fathers improve and develop healthy, loving relationships with their daughters. For those of you who are married, it is critical to the success of this commitment that you and your wife share similar philosophies and beliefs about raising your daughter.

Many couples marry, yet never really discuss the possibility of having children and how they would like to raise them. On the other hand, couples agree to have children but often fail to discuss fully all the important questions that come up:

When do we want to have children?
How many do we want to have?
How will we raise them, and what kind of sacrifices will we have to make?
Are we prepared for children?
Will one of us stay home with them, or will we use day care?
Will having children affect our careers?
How will they impact our finances, and how many can we afford to have?
Will our lives really change or will it resemble fairy tales, traditional stereotypes, or images of marriage we were exposed to by the media and society while growing up?

Don't you find it scary how many of us have had very little, if any, exposure to healthy, loving relationships while growing up, yet we don't take any of this into consideration before getting married and having children? We need a license to drive a car and a résumé to get a job, yet there are no mandatory prerequisites for having children. Somehow, this system just doesn't seem right, and our children and our society will continue to pay the price. Prior to getting married, adults should be required to take a course on marriage and raising children. At least then, we couldn't use excuses like "No one ever told me it would be this way," and "If I'd known it was going to be this way, I might've done things differently."

We can't go back and change the past, but we certainly can learn and grow from past experiences and better prepare ourselves for the future. Therefore, whether you're married right now (with or without children) or plan to be married and have children some day, please make sure you and your spouse thoroughly discuss your plans for raising your daughter. Make sure you have a clear understanding of each other's philosophy and beliefs, and then possibly you can come to a satisfactory compromise.

I feel strongly about people taking responsibility as parents, and that parents should raise their children together. That said, I realize there are circumstances and events in life that make it very difficult, if not impossible, at times for parents to raise their own children together, full-time. Still, too many parents don't have their priorities in order and have a tendency to take the easy way out by not designing a plan to be more involved in their children's lives. In some cases, I wonder why people even have children if they know they will spend so very little time with them. It's sad, but many people from different backgrounds and income levels adopt an irresponsible approach to having children and raising them. As parents, we must take responsibility for rearing our children and play active roles in their lives.

There are many premarital classes and programs offered at churches everywhere and independent programs as well. If you plan to get married, I encourage you to take advantage of them to help you better prepare for marriage and child rearing. All the money and material objects in the world will never help you to become a better father or ensure a lifelong healthy and loving relationship with your daughter. So make sure you plan well and that both you and your spouse are on the same page when deciding to have children.

Embrace Family Structure

Later in this chapter I write about how critical structure is in terms of discipline. If we embrace structure well before we start thinking about discipline, it makes the entire process easier on both fathers and daughters. Now we're ready to discuss how to develop and adapt to a family structure and to make sure the entire family not only embraces and embodies it, but sticks with it as well.

Would you agree, in general, a family is like

a sports team in that it's a group of people working together to achieve a common goal? Everyone plays a different role; some are better than others at certain things. If anyone needs help, usually there's somebody there to help out. A good team requires a coach, who provides leadership and a strong role model. This coach sets up the rules and boundaries for the team's structure and calls practices. The coach works with the players and sees to it that they have all the equipment they need, thereby giving them the best chance to succeed. When it's game time, as a team they hope they prepared well enough to win. In the end, they know it's unlikely to win every game, but if they keep working hard together, learning, and gaining more experience, they'll put themselves in a position to succeed more often than not.

On the other hand, there's this other team with poor leadership and a coach who doesn't really care much about the players. Players come and go as they please, and they don't respect the coach much because he clearly lacks leadership and dedication. There are no rules, no structure, teamwork, cooperation, communication, and very few practices. This team's eventual breakdown and confusion stems from poor coaching. You see where I'm going with this?

Which coach and team would you rather play for and be a part of? I assume most of you would choose the successful team, right? Why is that? Perhaps because, as much as some would tell you differently, everyone wants and embraces structure and good leadership and wants to be part of a winning team. If those two teams were families, which family would you want to be a part of? Your daughter will thrive on structure. She needs leadership, a role model, and balance in her life. She needs love. She needs a father who will take charge, provide clear boundaries, and work hard so the family not only embraces it, but sticks with it as well—and succeeds.

Now that we've covered the difference between good structure and no structure at all, I'd like to share some examples of a family structure my wife and I developed and adopted along the way with a great deal of success. Note that as I describe our family structure, it's not in any particular order or hierarchy. The goal is to give you a look at what has worked for us and share some ideas that you can then customize to your own family's needs.

Structure begins in the morning. During the school week, our daughters get up at 6:30 a.m. They dress in clothes they had picked out the night before in order to save time and hassle. My wife gets up about 6:00 a.m. and prepares breakfast and the girls' school lunches. Since my wife and I are concerned about our entire family getting the proper nutrition, she takes the time every morning to prepare healthy, nutritional breakfasts and lunches. These two important meals include a combination of well-balanced food—no sodas, candy, or potato chips. The girls have several different choices for breakfast, like oatmeal, cereal, eggs, waffles, cream of wheat, yogurt, protein shakes, or fruit. Usually they alternate the meals every morning so they're not eating the same thing every day. The girls are responsible for getting their homework and backpacks together, brushing their teeth, and feeding the dog before leaving for school.

When they get home from school, the girls do some homework. If they have piano or softball practice, they'll go to one or the other, and then do their homework after dinner. Since my wife is home during the day, she plans and prepares the meals so we eat as well as we can as a family. We eat dinner together maybe four or five weeknights and almost always on weekends. When I get home late or the girls have practice or some function they're attending, we obviously don't eat together. After dinner, the girls finish any homework they have and then read for forty-five minutes to an hour every night. Part of our family structure and rules is that our daughters don't watch television or play computer games during the school week, only on weekends, vacations, and holidays.

Unless homework keeps the girls up later than usual, they are in bed between 8:30–9:00 p.m. on school nights. On weekends, holidays, or vacations, we let them stay up until about ten o'clock or later, if they last that late. The girls brush their teeth every night before bed and lay out clothes for school the next day. Without fail, both girls ask my wife and me for a kiss goodnight before going to sleep, a routine that is very special to me. They don't want the kiss until they're in their beds and ready to go to sleep. It's been the same routine since they were two or three years old. Our daughters are also responsible for making their beds every day, picking up their rooms, and completing various chores around the house.

This daily routine is simple and systematic. That's our basic, daily family structure, and we do a pretty good job at sticking to it. The key is repetition and consistency. It instills in our daughters good eating habits, good sleeping habits, good study habits, good hygiene, good practice habits, and age-appropriate responsibility. Please evaluate your current family structure and see if you need to make any adjustments. If not, that's great. If so, sit down by yourself or with your spouse and work at developing and adopting a new or better family structure. Once you have a plan, embrace it and stick to it, because it will pay huge dividends for your daughter and the entire family.

SLOW DOWN!

Families just don't seem to have much of a connection or cohesiveness these days, probably because they're so busy all the time. Wouldn't you agree that if you were to observe a cross-section of families' daily activities, chances are that many of them would be filled with chaos, confusion, and mayhem? If you haven't done so already, I encourage you to stand aside and observe the daily routines of other families. Then, after making your observations, take a long look at your own family and daily routine.

Of course, all of our families and lives get crazy and chaotic at times; nothing's perfect in life. Nevertheless, for too many families this chaos is an everyday occurrence. I'm not referring to families where both parents have to scramble from one job to another, because they can't make ends meet financially and struggle to buy food and clothes for their children. I'm talking about the typical baby boomer family in mid- or high-income brackets. They probably own or rent a home in a nice neighborhood and own one or two cars, maybe even a boat or vacation home.

In a nutshell, they're doing fine financially and enjoying comfortable or above-average lifestyles with one or both parents working to generate income. That's our demographic model. So why are most of us in such a hurry, never slowing down, rushed and frantic most of the time? Everyone has a theory or belief as to how and why this accelerated lifestyle has swept so many of us up and how it has impacted society.

Here's my take on the matter: Quite simply, it's all up to us as parents. That's right. We are responsible for this pedal-to-the-metal lifestyle. Here's the reality: If your family life seems to be too hurried or out of control most of the time, I suggest you make time to figure out how you and your spouse or partner allowed it to get that way. We could blame our jobs or our children, our children's schools, or after-school activities. We could blame modern society by saying, "That's just the way it is. Everyone's living like this, not just us." The reality is, parents, in almost every case, are completely responsible for how their families operate, crazy or not. Parents make the decisions. We decide whether one or both of us needs or wants to work. We decide whether we want a more expensive home or not. We decide whether we want a new car every few years. We decide whether we want to have one, two, three, or four children. We decide whether our children participate in one or several sports or activities at a time, in any given time. We decide whether or not to take the time to cook and eat healthy. We decide to charge up credit cards and add to our stress. We decide whether or not to establish and stick to a budget.

I think you get the message. If a family's lifestyle is hectic and frenzied, the parents are to blame—not the children or anyone else. After all, we're the ones who decided to start a family to begin with. We make the choices and have control over most of them. So what do we do to change the situation, slow it down, or make adjustments so we can get a somewhat normal life back? Well, there are a few things we can do if we really care enough about our family environment.

First, schedule some quiet time with your spouse when the children aren't around; this might take a few meetings or maybe a weekend away. Have an open and honest conversation about the way you're doing things now. Identify the things that are causing the most problems or stress.

Ask yourselves questions like:

Are we working too much, and if so, why?
Are we spending too much money, so we're forced to earn more?
Are the children involved in too many sports or activities at one time?
If so, why do we have them in so many?

Is it because that's what they want, or because is it what we want?

Is it because that's what we think they want?

Suppose I rush my daughter to piano lessons right after school for an hour, then rush like crazy to get her to softball practice, and then hurry her home to cram two hours worth of homework into an hour. Then we miss dinner, and all of us are stressed out because this takes place three days a week. Is it really fun and enjoyable for her or for us, or is it just frustrating and crazy? Are any of these types of activities productive, positive, or pleasurable under these circumstances? Probably not, and if not, what can we do about it?

In this case, we might discuss the following: What if we just stayed in this smaller house for a while longer, didn't take on a bigger mortgage payment, and didn't buy that new car we wanted? That way, one of us could work less, and we'd have more time and save money. Yes, and maybe we could even eat dinner together more often. Yes, and maybe if both children were only in one sport or activity at a given time, we could spend more family time together, having fun and enjoying each other's company, as we used to do. Remember?

Here's another possible scenario: A family has plenty of income and financial resources, and only one parent has to work. Yet even with that luxury, for some reason the family is still in a frantic state regularly. It's not always about the money and the pressure of making ends meet. Why is that? It's because, for the most part, it has nothing to do with money and everything to do with the parent or parents. Perhaps we feel more important when we're busy, or we need to stay busy to avoid having to deal with personal issues we'd rather not confront. Maybe we feel pressure to keep up with others in society. We want so badly for our children to succeed at something in life that we have them enrolled in multiple sports or activities. Possibly, we don't feel comfortable in our own skin, and we keep searching for whatever it is that will make us happy. It could be that unless we're succeeding in business or accumulating additional wealth or assets, we feel less important or accomplished.

Countless reasons exist for our behaviors. Please understand that I'm not suggesting that there's anything wrong with being successful or accumulating wealth. Actually, it's extremely important for all of us to feel successful at something in life. We also need to continue trying to be a better person and parent. We must do all of these things for the right reasons, ones that don't come at a cost to our relationships with the people we love and care about. Some people say, "Money is evil. It ruins people and changes them." I disagree. Money doesn't change people, make them evil, or ruin their lives. People do that to themselves, because they can't handle the additional money or the responsibility that comes with success. There's nothing wrong with money or success. It's all about striking a balance between all of the important things in life.

The key is not to waste time blaming each other or making excuses why you can't get better control over your family. Address the situation like a healthy adult. Sit down and talk about it, and figure out the best strategy for you and your family. Don't be concerned about what other people are saying or doing. Set aside one day a week, twice a month, or whatever works where the entire family enjoys the day together with no plans at all. Choose just to be lazy all day, take a bike ride, or go to the beach. Your daughters are young only once, and you don't ever get another chance to spend time with them as three-year-olds, as four-year-olds, or as kids. Period.

Structure and Discipline

Questions like whether to spank or not, whether timeouts actually work, and if they do, at what age do you stop, etc. are always going to be cause for debate and controversy. I firmly believe the approach each of us takes to disciplining our daughter starts way before she's even born. After she's born, discipline evolves along the way, depending on the extent of work we do as fathers.

As we become adults and prepare for children, unless we make an effort to research and better understand child development, we will simply administer discipline on the fly. Many of us will most likely resort back to and rely on our learned behavior and will really have no structure for administering discipline. We don't suddenly become parents and have this magical ability bestowed upon us. Until we did it for the first time, I bet most of us never thought much at all about how we wanted to discipline our daughters.

It starts younger than most of us imagine. The structure starts to form when your infant daughter has to adjust to feeding times, nap times, or sleeping in her own crib.

The point here is that the sooner we have a plan, set the stage, take charge, and make the rules, the sooner the actual act of disciplining starts. Even before all of that, ask yourself if you have a plan. Are you going to take the time to educate yourself about child development and do some research and talk to other parents who appear to have had some success in this area? If you're married, are you going to talk to your spouse about each other's philosophy and beliefs and how you want to go about disciplining your young daughter? These are important questions that healthy, committed parents should be asking themselves before having children, yet many of us don't.

I enjoy hypothetical situations, so let me pose a few for you and see what you think. Let's say you had the most important test in your life to study for, one that meant getting your degree or not. Would you study the appropriate material until you knew it extremely well? Alternatively, would you not worry about it, show up, and take your chances on the test without studying? On the other hand, let's say you're a baseball player. The game is everything to you, and you have a chance to become a major league player and sign a multi-million-dollar contract. The only thing that stands in your way is that you have to improve your defense, by fielding ground balls better. Would you go out and make sure you took as many ground balls as it took to improve your defense, or would you simply hope to get better? I could go on forever about the importance of preparation, about applying yourself the best ways you know possible for something this important in your life. So I ask you this: Is your baby girl important enough to you to be sure you're prepared to administer structure and discipline to her, or will you just wait and see what happens?

Now let's move on to my philosophy and strategies for discipline once your little girl is born. First, as I mentioned earlier, please make sure you set the stage as early as possible by providing structure. Two of the biggest challenges in the early years are scheduled nap times and getting your daughter to sleep in her own crib. The sooner you enforce the nap times and stick with them, the easier it will be going forward. Sometimes your little girl won't want to take a nap, or she may not seem like she's ready. However, even if she's not ready or willing, it's up to us as fathers to stick to the set times. Even if she just lays there, cries, or throws a fit, the best thing to do is make sure she knows this is the time. Whether she naps or not, she will stay in the bed and in the room during the entire time she's supposed to be napping.

As difficult as it can be, and I know because I've been there, we need to stick to the plan and the schedule. Even if she lies in her bed and cries for thirty minutes or more, you mustn't give in. You might feel as if you're abusing your little girl, but these are the battles you must win. As soon as you give in and let her run the show and dictate the schedule for you, you've lost control. Your daughter will control you. It sounds funny, but it's true. At that early age, she will have full control over what she wants and when, unless you remain steadfast.

You could have another battle on your hands when your little girl doesn't want to sleep in her crib or bed. This is also extremely difficult to manage at times because she might cry herself to sleep or get so upset that, once again, you feel like it's a form of child abuse. However, it will pay off in the long run, and that's what you must keep in mind while going through these trying times. I can remember more than a few times when my wife and I were sitting in the living room crying ourselves because our daughter didn't want to sleep in her crib and wouldn't stop crying and was throwing some of the biggest fits we'd ever heard. Sure enough, after a period of time, the crying stopped. After a few episodes, she ended up being a great sleeper and continued sleeping through the night. Both daughters went through the same struggle and discipline, and both are solid sleepers to this day.

The next challenging stages came at the ages of two and between five and six, when we adopted timeouts as a form of discipline. This system worked well for us, but not until after both daughters fought the program vigorously and finally realized we weren't going to give in. I want to make something very clear about discipline in our family, and I'll be completely honest. Because my wife has been home with our daughters since they were born, she's the one who's had to dish out most of the discipline. She's fought more battles, and she deserves the most credit. I've always done as much as I could when I was home, but it wasn't quite the same. Those who are full-time with the children and are committed and dedicated parents have the most difficult job there is.

When our girls were around six years old, we had to scrap the timeout program, because it no longer worked. We had to increase the consequences for inappropriate behavior. Since they were old enough to enjoy certain foods, shows, games, and activities, we learned through our pediatrician and from reading up on the subject that the take-away program would be more effective and still is to this day. Therefore, any time the girls required disciplining, we took something away for a period of time, depending on how severe the grievance was. For example, if the grievance was something minor, we might not let them watch a show they really liked to watch on Saturday nights. If the grievance was worse, we might not allow any of their friends to come over for a week or two. If it was even more serious, we might forbid two or three of their favorite activities for a month.

Another form of discipline we've used for the past few years, in addition to the take-away, is writing. We have them write a paragraph or two about what they did or said that was wrong, and most important, what they are going to do in the future to prevent it from happening again. For instance, suppose Rachel gets mad and hits Stephanie or throws something at her that could hurt her. We'd take something away from Rachel for a period of time and also have her write about it. In her writing, she would have to write about how sorry she was for hitting her sister and how she realizes it was wrong and that we don't treat people we care about this way. The next time she gets mad, she will try to walk away or tell her sister why she's mad instead of hitting her. I especially like the writing discipline because it makes the girls sit down, replay in their minds what they did wrong, write it down, and see it in print.

Another critical component in any type of discipline is trying to stay calm and adult-like when addressing the problem. We've all been there and know what it's like when we get upset or have just had enough. We blow up, yell at our children, or even spank or hit them. We aren't perfect, but is this really the healthy, adult way to handle any situation? Of course it's not. And after we cool down, most of us realize we were wrong by reacting that way. We'd probably admit to being a bit embarrassed or ashamed.

The bottom line is that as parents and grown adults, we need to lead by example and handle these potentially volatile situations the best way possible. More important, we should always explain to our young daughters why we got upset and apologize if we feel we didn't handle the situation properly. As parents, we need to apologize when we make mistakes, for two reasons: First, because we should, and it's the right thing to do if we were wrong. Second, it teaches our daughters that they should also apologize if they are wrong or make a mistake. Much of parenting is leading by example. Sometimes we get so caught up in the moment or in who's right and who's wrong, we tend to forget that we should turn these situations into learning experiences for our daughters and ourselves.

Numerous thoughts and philosophies exist regarding how children should be disciplined. Some are driven by religious beliefs—some by what our parents did or didn't do when we were children. I suspect most people don't really know why they discipline a certain way. There are parents who don't discipline at all and feel it's the best approach. Others go to the opposite extreme and feel spanking, hitting, and yelling are best. I try not to make any judgments or tell people their way is wrong. I might disagree with the way someone disciplines, but I'd never say my way is the right way or the only way. However, I would hope that I could have a conversation with others about this topic, and they'd likewise respect my views, without being judgmental. Personally, I don't think any form of physical discipline, like spanking or hitting, can have any positive results for a young child. That said, I'm not talking about parents losing control from time to time and lightly swatting their children on the bottom. No, that's much different than if someone has a philosophy of discipline where spanking or hitting is the norm and the first resort rather than the last. The logic behind this kind of disciplining just doesn't make any sense to me. Let me explain why.

If I were to get mad at someone in my office, at one of my friends or a neighbor, and I wanted to teach them a lesson for upsetting me or doing something wrong, should I hit them? Most people would say absolutely not, and if you did, you could be arrested and maybe thrown in jail. Therefore,

I could never understand the logic behind continually spanking or hitting a child as a form of discipline. Some might counter my position and argue that the situation's different because these are children and not adults, and they don't know the difference between right and wrong. As parents, it's our job to teach them, and the best way to get their attention and teach them right from wrong—to get the quickest results—is to spank or hit them. I'm still not buying it. I've tried to be as open-minded as I can and have yet to see where physical contact, violence, or abuse can work in any child's favor.

One form of discipline used just as much if not more than the others is so-called verbal discipline. Parents often resort to yelling or raising their voices and think it's okay because they're not spanking or hitting their children. However, this can be even more damaging than physical discipline. Those who scream and yell at their children also have a tendency to berate and demean them in the process. This can be very hurtful and cause long-term problems for children, as they grow older. I'm a bit too familiar with verbal abuse because both my parents used it on a regular basis with my siblings and me, and our parents went back and forth berating each other as well. To this day, I have to work hard at times to stop from raising my voice when I get upset. The difference for me now is that when I do raise my voice on rare occasion, my wife or my daughters immediately bring it to my attention, and I'm a lot better about apologizing right away.

I hope these examples and suggestions help

illustrate just how important the topic of discipline is. You really need to think about how you'll prepare yourself before your daughter is born. If she's already born, think about how you might make some adjustments. Know that it's never too late to be open to new ideas and different philosophies or to make changes if it makes sense, especially when your relationship with your daughter depends on it.

To summarize the very complicated and controversial subject of discipline, I'd like to explain something I truly believe. Fathers, if we focus more on structure during the early years instead of looking at it as discipline, it might make more sense. Loving and caring structure sets the stage early on and teaches our daughters who is in charge and who makes the rules. If you begin with that, discipline will become much easier. In addition to structure, put your time and energy into explaining to your daughter the difference between right and wrong, and as much as you can, about what's in between.

Remember, when disciplining, try to talk about the behavior instead of the person. Too often, we get mad at our little girls and refer to them as the problem, when we really should refer to their behavior as the problem. Of course, the main ingredient is to love her unconditionally and spend time with her. Learn to build mutual trust and respect with her, talk to her, and include her in your life. Never stop telling her how much you love her. If you focus on these types of activities, believe me, the discipline will be a lot easier on both of you.

Rituals and Routines

I'm a big believer in rituals and routines, not only for families, but for individuals, for businesses, for organizations, and for sports teams as well. If we establish these two important structures in our lives in a positive way, they can be tremendous benefits. On the other hand, if we establish either one in a negative way, we'll reap more problems than benefits.

So here's what works for us. Please note that this list of family rituals and routines is in no hierarchical order.

- We eat dinner together almost every evening.
- We hold family meetings at least once a month.
- We schedule monthly dates for my wife and me.
- We have monthly one-on-one dates with one parent and one of the girls.
- We take scheduled vacations together at least three times a year.
- We only allow a limited amount of TV on weekends, holidays, and vacations. No TV is allowed during the school week.
- We have scheduled reading time.
- We continually talk about the importance of good eating habits.
- We continually talk about the importance of physical fitness and exercise.
- We cook and bake together.

- We enter the girls in only one sport and one other activity at a time.
- We attend all school functions designed for parent participation.
- The girls and I make hot chocolate every Saturday morning.
- The girls and I will make breakfast together almost every weekend.
- We do yard work together as a family.
- Every morning before school, I tell the girls to have an F. and S. D. This is our code for them to have a Fun and Smart Day!
- We pray together.
- We do an indoor or outdoor activity together every weekend.
- My wife will take the girls, so I can do something by myself or with family or friends.
- I will take the girls, so my wife can do something by herself or with family or friends.
- Relatives or friends will take the girls, so my wife and I can do something together.
- My wife works with the girls on the piano.
- My wife and I both work with the girls on their sports, including coaching.
- Once a week, we will all lie together and watch a show on TV or a movie.
- If I'm in town, I attend every one of my daughters' games, school events, plays, piano recitals, etc.

• We talk to our daughters about business and entrepreneurship on a regular basis.
• We talk to our daughters about money, finances, and investing on a regular basis.
• We continually point out and give examples to our daughters when people do good things for others out of kindness and compassion.
• We continually point out and give examples to our daughters when others demonstrate leadership, good values, or good judgment.
• Unless we have something specifically planned, we let the girls choose what they want to do or where they want to go on weekends, holidays, and vacations.
• We continually remind the girls about the true value of quality friends and family members who care about us.
• We teach our daughters that they should be kind and respectful people, and they should also expect the same from others.
• We talk to our daughters all the time about finding something they love to do or for which they have a passion and how success will follow.

These are a good sampling of our family rituals and routines. They've worked well for us. We firmly believe in our approach to parenting and the love and compassion that go with it. Having said that, please understand that even though these have worked for us, we're better at some than others. Some of them don't always go the way we like, but we just do the best we can and keep learning along the way. Some fathers might find them useful; others might want to change them a bit. Even better, try to create a list of your own from scratch. Either way, these types of family rituals and routines can be both fun and extremely rewarding for fathers, their daughters, and the entire family.

Work | Life Balance

Without proper balance in our lives, we could never spend the necessary time with our families or our daughters. We hear so many people talk about how important work and life balance is, yet I'm not sure how many people really apply it successfully in their daily lives. It's so easy to get caught up in our jobs or our businesses, finances, homes, school, sports, and other activities. Where do we draw the line, and how do we get it all done without compromising the time we need to spend with our daughters?

The first thing you should do is just stop moving so fast for a few days; take some time to sit down with your spouse or by yourself and reflect. Reflect and refocus on what is important to you, your family, and your daughter. Ask yourself questions like: Why am I working, and am I working too much? Well, I need money, so I have to work, but am I working just to survive or is there a meaning or purpose to what I'm doing? I'm getting a bit philosophical here, but please stay with me. Many of us get caught up working or doing something to generate income at some stage of our lives because we have to. However, are we really doing what we want to in our job or career? Is it because we think we need to? I'm not suggesting that you quit your job, sell your business, or do something drastic if you find yourself questioning whether you're doing the right thing. However, if you're not happy with your job or business, take some time to evaluate your current situation; think about what you actually might want to do. This doesn't have to happen overnight, but you should continue spending the necessary time exploring other opportunities until you feel as if you're making progress.

You might be wondering what all of this has to do with work | life balance. Well, it has everything to do with balance. The reason is that if you're the primary income earner and you're not satisfied professionally, it will have a negative effect on other aspects of your life, including your relationship with your daughter.

Remember, the goal in this part of the chapter is to really focus on the area of work | life balance and find out what we're doing and why. If we can do this, we can figure out where we're spending our time and energy. Once this is accomplished, we can make the necessary adjustments to be sure we're spending our time in the areas that need it most. Again, if you're married, talk to your spouse and to your daughter about it as well, if she's at least six or seven years old. If she's any younger, it's probably not the proper age or time.

As a father, whether you feel you're on the right career path or not, you should evaluate on a daily basis where you're spending your time, and make sure you spend some of it with your daughter. It's not that your career, your personal life, and your relationship with your spouse aren't important, because they are, obviously. Your relationship with your little girl is also extremely important, and she needs you more than you know. You must balance your daily activities so that she isn't left out. If you're struggling and finding it difficult to achieve a balance, I encourage you to seek a personal coach, read books on this topic, or find a friend or family member who can help.

Equally important for a successful work/life balance for fathers is personal time. Make time for things you enjoy, including your favorite hobbies and activities. Whether it's time at the gym, golfing, swimming, riding a bike, sailing, or whatever, make sure you allow time for yourself. Remember, we're talking about balance, so don't confuse personal time with trying to justify something like watching sports on television all weekend and ignoring your daughter. I enjoy following sports as much as the next guy, and there's nothing wrong with watching TV here and there, alone, or with others. Moderation and balance are the keys.

I'm not just picking on sports either; fathers can easily justify spending more hours at work or out with their buddies or on business trips too. There are all sorts of potential distractions and diversions. It's your decision. Do you want your daughter to grow up without you, even though you live together, or do you want to be part of her life?

CHAPTER 7
Words and Actions—Choose Wisely

I'm sure you're familiar with the saying, "Actions speak louder than words." Well, as a father, *both* your words and actions speak very loudly and are extremely powerful, so choose them carefully.

This is one of the most difficult and challenging areas for a father. From the time your daughter is born, she listens to the things you say and witnesses what you do. No matter your daughter's age, this is always a concern. Even more so during the first five or six years when she's developing her personality and character and a relationship with you. Our young daughters are virtually little tape recorders and video cameras. They mentally store what they hear and see and will likely repeat much of it. Of course, without fail they repeat some of the negative or inappropriate things you've done or said at the most inopportune times.

Most parents are familiar with this situation: You're driving down the road with your daughter and another car cuts in front of you, so you say, "You jerk" or something worse.

Then about three days later as you're driving down the road with your daughter again, your daughter looks over at the car next to you and for no reason says, "You jerk."

You immediately get a bit upset and ask,

"Why did you say that? Where did you hear that?"

Your daughter replies, "You said it, Daddy." You experience a sinking feeling when you realize she probably heard you say it the other day while driving. Bingo!

Consider the adage, "Do as I say, not as I do." That's a great one, isn't it? No wonder our daughters get confused. Fathers, if you get angry and yell, scream, or curse, is it okay if your daughter does the same when she gets angry? Do you see what I'm getting at? This happens all too often with parents, and many times we don't see what we're doing unless someone brings it to our attention or we're alert enough to catch it ourselves. We can't expect our young daughters to accept this type of double standard. Instead, we must work extremely hard at watching what we say and what we do in front of them.

None of us are perfect, so when these unfortunate situations arise and you're guilty of a double standard, make sure you sit down with your daughter and discuss the matter. Apologize, and then explain to her that what you did wasn't appropriate—as her father, you realize you didn't set a very good example.

The key here is to pay close attention to what you say and how you conduct yourself around your daughter and others. My wife and I are constantly talking to our girls about what's right and what's wrong, what's appropriate and what's not. We're also aware that they're exposed to environments outside our home, so we discuss with them the way they should conduct themselves as individuals when elsewhere.

Take the extra time to evaluate your choice of words and actions, specifically when they relate to your daughter. For example, please refrain from expressions like "bad girl" or "Only bad girls do that." Many parents still scold like this because these expressions were used with them and around them while growing up. They are very negative terms and a harmful choice of words. The word *bad* implies that your daughter is a bad person for doing something wrong. Is your daughter really a bad person because she did something wrong or upset you? Of course not, and if you repeatedly call your daughter bad when she does something wrong or misbehaves, it sends the wrong message. Think for a moment about the word bad. It's negative and vague. Instead, when your daughter does something wrong, try for example something like the following: "That is unacceptable behavior in our home. We don't treat people like that." You might say something like "We don't use words like that. That was inappropriate. How do you think the person felt when you made that mean comment?" These are all good alternatives to saying, "You're a bad girl." Be very specific about the action, condemn the behavior rather than her as a person, and stick to the topic. Moreover, never forget to explain to your daughter why you are upset with her and what the consequences are for her behavior.

There are a variety of negative words and actions that are easy to use when we get mad, upset, or disappointed. There are also many positive ways to handle these same situations. The best way is to rehearse and try to anticipate many of them. Take yourself through a routine or find someone to help you rehearse. If you're married, rehearse with your spouse as well. Imagine a scenario that has come up before that you wish you'd handled differently. Now visualize that scenario over and over, the way you want to handle it next time. Practice this type of successful visualization with as many different scenarios as possible. Work hard at trying to respond rather than reacting, and choose your words and actions very carefully.

Be a Role Model

We hear people talk about positive role models and how important they are to our young children. The problem is, many times we make references to athletes, movie stars, entertainers, and others as role models. Don't get me wrong—I'm sure some of these people referred to are wonderful and respectful human beings. However, how can we label and categorize these people without really knowing them? How can we say to our daughter, "Now she's a great role model for girls," when we don't know that person? It's not fair to that person, and it's certainly not a responsible thing to say to your daughter. If my daughter looks up to or idealizes someone, that's her choice. Although, as a responsible parent, I owe it to her to explain that until we really know someone we truly don't know what kind of a person he or she is. It's a matter of integrity versus accomplishment.

As fathers, we should conduct our lives as if we were the ultimate male role models for our daughters. Does this mean we should be perfect, have all the answers, or suggest our daughters not have other role models? Absolutely not, but what I do suggest is that we continue to raise the bar when it comes to setting an example for our young daughters as to how a father should conduct himself personally and professionally. This includes the way in which you navigate your life and communicate with both men and women. If you take a responsible and overall positive approach to life and treat both men and women with mutual respect, the chances are this will impact your daughter's life, and she will remember this about you. How do you react and respond to issues of adversity and life-defining events? If you stay somewhat balanced and objective, chances are, your daughter will remember this about you as well—the way you manage your family, your relationships, and the way you approach life. If you continue to work hard at being a well-balanced, compassionate person and an active and responsible father, all of these factors will determine whether your daughter grows up viewing you as a positive and healthy role model.

We can't be obsessed with how our daughters will think and feel about us as they get older. However, we owe it to them to set the stage and to demonstrate how a responsible and caring father conducts himself and his life for their betterment.

No Stereotypes

I have already touched on the topic of gender stereotypes, but I feel it's important enough to warrant a short section with more detailed information and examples. There's such a wide range and different degrees of gender stereotyping in society that fathers must be alert to the warning signs. I'll discuss some of the obvious and not so obvious stereotypes and how to avoid their potentially negative impact on our daughters.

Some obvious stereotyping occurs at home, school, and work. At home, we need to be aware of the seemingly innocent notions that boys are more interested in sports than girls, and that girls really don't need to worry about money or finances because when they get married their husbands will take care of them. As a father, let's say I handle all the financial matters in the family: planning a budget, paying bills, investing in a college plan for my daughters, investing in a retirement plan, etc. In addition, I never share this information with my wife or my daughters or offer to involve them. The message I'm sending is that financial responsibility is strictly for men. Suppose I have a son and a daughter, and I love golf and automatically assume that my son wants to learn the game, but my daughter doesn't. Granted, this kind of bias has declined somewhat over time. However, you'd be surprised to find out how many fathers, who have both girls and boys, still have a tendency to spend more time with their sons when it comes to sports or other traditionally male activities.

Let's take a look at the potential issues that

could arise when a father stereotypes in matters of sports and finance. By not exposing our young daughters to either financial responsibility or the game of golf, we are doing a lot more damage than just assuming that they wouldn't be interested in becoming a financial advisor or professional golfer. We are potentially suppressing our young daughters' opportunities to express and demonstrate their unique abilities and talents in these activities as well as others. When we label people or automatically rule them out without really knowing what they are capable of, we never really know what they can do. Think about it, are we really qualified to decide for our eight-year-old daughter that she won't be interested in sports or finance? No, we're not. Therefore, please be mindful of these types of seemingly innocent biases.

I was reminded of the potential dangers in labeling and stereotyping with my young daughter Stephanie just about two years ago. Stephanie was just turning seven at the time and after watching her older sister play softball for the past two years; she was looking forward to playing herself. Leading up to her deciding to play softball, I would mention to my wife from time to time. "I'm not sure Stephanie will enjoy herself playing softball because she appears to get bored easily and softball can be a boring sport for some, especially at the age of seven and eight." I never discussed or expressed these thoughts with Stephanie or ever discouraged her from playing softball. However, I was somewhat convinced that she would most likely not be interested in playing softball. Well, strike one giant life lesson up for Dad! Stephanie not only loved playing her first year, but she learned the game quickly and made remarkable progress. Now entering her second year, she eats, drinks, and sleeps softball and not only loves the game, but is extremely good at it for her age as well.

What do you suppose would have happened if I had openly and verbally expressed my opinions and thoughts about softball with Stephanie? We won't ever know, but what if I did express my feelings to her and it discouraged her from ever playing softball? What if Stephanie figured her father knew best, and if I was convinced softball wasn't for her, she never ended up playing? I get emotional writing about this, just thinking about the power and influence we have over our young daughters and how scary it could be if we're not mindful of this as fathers.

Try to expose your young daughter to as many aspects of life as possible, whether it's business, sports, music, art, etc. Don't assume she's not interested until she's been exposed to it and tells you so. When my daughters reached seven years old, I had them sit down with me when I paid the bills and explained to them what I was doing and why we have to pay bills. I also let them put the stamps on the envelopes and file statements for me. These types of activities help to keep them involved and having fun! They have their own bank accounts, know about their college saving plans, and have a general understanding of our family investments. My wife and I have introduced our daughters to a variety of sports, music, and theater. They play the piano, softball, and participate in drama, and they enjoy them all very much.

Two other examples of gender stereotypes to be aware of are in the areas of education and business. We should continually talk to our young daughters about the doors a good education opens and the many career choices available to them. Talk to them about successful women in the business world and in professional sports, as well as the successful mothers who dedicate their time to their family and children. Talk to them about the different business opportunities out there, about starting their own businesses, and about entrepreneurship. We fathers must steer our daughters away from stereotypes and make them aware of their options, no matter what anyone else says or thinks.

Real Equality

I touched on this topic in the section about avoiding gender stereotypes, but it warrants another look. Some very alarming statistics and surveys indicate that, on the whole, fathers would rather raise sons. Conditions have improved over the past few decades, but girls and women are still discriminated against on many different levels in numerous areas, including education and business. In many cases, they are not afforded the same opportunities as boys and men. Consciously or subconsciously, many fathers might condone this type of behavior.

An article appeared in *Money Magazine*

titled, "Girls Not Welcome: Men would rather raise sons than daughters, which has financial consequences for the whole family." To quote the article: "Surveys have shown that while American women are just as happy to have girl babies as boys, American fathers stubbornly prefer sons to daughters by a margin of more than two to one." "According to a study by two economists, Gordon Dahl of the University of Rochester and Enrico Moretti of UCLA, including data pulled from hospitals, birth certificates and census records, parents with girls only were more likely to be divorced, and divorced dads were more likely to have custody of their sons than of their daughters. In the case of "Shotgun marriages," the economists found that men were far more likely to marry the mothers of their children when the ultrasounds revealed that the babies were boys. Additional findings by the same economists also say some Americans are so set on a boy that they just keep on having kids— and ringing up all the expenses that come with them—until a son finally arrives."[2]

Keep in mind, this article was written primarily to show the financial implications of parents who continually have children until they have a boy. Just the same, the article also points out some alarming statistics about the way many men think and feel when it comes to boys and girls.

There are reams of articles that document how fathers treat or perceive their daughters versus their sons, but let's look at just a few. A recent article, "Why Some Fathers Don't Relate to Their Daughters," states that "Even before daughters are born, many fathers feel conflicted.

A Gallup poll conducted recently showed that 45% of men would prefer having a son if they had only one child, compared with 19% who'd prefer a daughter–a ratio little changed since 1941."[3] Once the girl arrives, her parents are more likely to get divorced than if she were a boy, according to a new study by researchers at the University of California at Los Angeles and the University of Rochester. Parents with three daughters are more likely to get divorced than parents with three sons. In homes with teenage girls, the likelihood of divorce doubles. Why are dads with sons less apt to divorce? They may feel a greater need to stick around as a male role model. They're also more comfortable around boys.

Please don't misunderstand me—boys need their fathers just as girls do. Yet sadly, many men still have the idea that it's more important for them to have a relationship with and be a role model for their sons than their daughters. This antiquated notion couldn't be further from the truth, and by this stage in the book, my guess is most fathers realize it by now. Your daughters need you just as much as your sons, and you could probably make a very good case as to why they need you even more.

If you're a father, I suggest you set aside some time to reflect—first by yourself, then with your spouse, to think about and discuss how you're currently raising your son and daughter. Try to determine as honestly as you can whether you're treating them differently. If you are, in what ways and in what areas? Are you spending more time with your son than with your daughter? Are you treating them differently when it comes to school, sports, business, or other activities, such as household chores? What types of activities are you participating in with your son and daughter? Are they the same or different ones? As your son and daughter get older, will you talk about and share a lot of the same things?

The questions above are intended to get you thinking about this topic and to determine whether or not you might be showing a little or a lot of preferential treatment to either your son or daughter. If not, that's great and you should be extremely proud of yourself. Keep up the great work. If any of the instances above apply to you, take the time to reexamine your father/son and father/daughter relationships. The good news is that if you discover you've been treating your son differently than your daughter, it's never too late to learn, make adjustments, and change. The even better news is that everyone around you, including your spouse, your daughter, and your son will eventually admire and respect you for acknowledging something so important and working on it.

Preferential treatment of boys over girls is often subtle and seemingly innocent, and it's not limited to us parents. This behavior exists and is prevalent among our relatives, friends, and co-workers and is found in schools, in workplaces, and in society at large. It starts with little things like your brother buying a set of golf clubs for your son on Christmas and buying your daughter a tea set. Alternatively, your sister buys your son building blocks for his birthday and buys your daughter a Barbie Doll® for hers. Your boss invites you and your son to a baseball game, but never even mentions or wonders if your daughter might be interested. Your sister-in-law calls your daughter and says, "Let's go have a girls day together and go shopping for some cute clothes, get our nails done, and get a pedicure." Your father (your children's grandfather) calls to invite his grandson fishing, and when they return with their catch, Grandma and her granddaughter (your daughter) cook the fish for dinner.

Again, don't misunderstand me, there's absolutely nothing wrong with the above activities or the way people addressed the boys. The real problem is that over the years these people have been conditioned to think that way about boys and girls, and they are making the mistake of assuming that girls aren't interested in the same things as boys. Well, maybe they are and maybe they aren't. It depends on the individual. What's important is that we make the same options available to both sexes.

Now let me be very clear; it would also be wrong to assume boys don't want to do certain things as well. So don't confuse this with the fact that there are still very powerful stereotypes in our society regarding girls and boys. The only way to change this pattern in our society is, for us fathers to commit to changing these patterns in our own homes. Once we've done the work at home, we can begin to influence others around us in the neighborhood, the community, and ultimately the country. How can we do this? We can do this by being a voice and promoting equality through father and daughter organizations. We can also be a voice for equality at school and in the workplace as well. If we want to raise awareness, fathers need to do more to make sure our daughters and sons are being treated equally everywhere and on every level.

A Father's View

This can be a challenging area and a difficult one to understand and acknowledge. It's confusing for many fathers because it's natural for them to love, adore, and respect their little girls. Still, in many cases, the way they treat and view other females can be completely opposite of the way they do their daughters.

Some fathers might feel a little uncomfortable with this topic and chapter. Most likely because we're human, we're men, and we're not perfect. Being no different than women, we tend to practice a double standard in certain areas of our lives—myself included. As fathers, it's not good to love and respect just our daughters; it's equally important to demonstrate to them that we respect other girls and women, treat them equally, and perceive them in an appropriate manner. A father is one of the most important, if not *the* most important role model, in his young daughter's life; her perception of him stems from how he treats and views other females. It's extremely critical, and it could very well mean the difference between a loving, healthy father-daughter relationship and a failed one.

The range of examples I might provide runs from subtle and seemingly innocent to extreme and potentially more damaging. Let's say you have inappropriate magazines, videos, or video games lying around the house or garage that depict girls or women as sex objects. How do you think your young daughter perceives these, and more to the point, what does she think about you? What about posters or pictures in your garage, home, or office featuring half-naked women in inappropriate, suggestive positions? Maybe you take your young daughter to a friend's house, and he has posters, videos, or magazines with inappropriate material. Suppose you take your daughter to a sports bar where there are various beer ads and posters on the walls with women in similar poses. Okay, okay, are you starting to see a pattern develop?

Fathers, we knowingly, or I'd hope unknowingly, send messages in many different ways to our young daughters. These messages are that females (just like our daughters) are more popular and appealing when scantily clad and seem to be here simply for man's viewing pleasure and entertainment. This kind of constant overexposure and demeaning portrayal of women will lead your daughter to believe that this is what all men want and expect from females, including her. Even worse, she'll assume this is what her father thinks and feels about them because he condones this type of material and behavior, and it's part of his lifestyle. Think about this. On Music Television (MTV), 75% of the videos that tell a story include sexual imagery, over 50% involve violence, and

80% combine the two, suggesting violence against women.[4]

Let me be brutally honest and plead with fathers. If you live this type of lifestyle, practice the behavior discussed above, continue to condone it in any way, shape, or form, and expose your daughter to it, you will ruin your chances of developing a healthy, loving relationship with her. However, even worse, it could influence whether she grows up to be sexually or physically abused by men or if she will fall into sexual promiscuity, prostitution, or pornography. This sounds harsh, but are you really willing to take the chance to have any of this happen?

I'd venture to say that most of us men, if we were being honest with each other, would admit to engaging in similar activities at one time or another in our lives, maybe before we were married or after—before we had our daughters or after. It doesn't matter. This book and chapter were never intended as an indictment of anyone or to cast blame or shame. The intent is to openly and honestly deal with the day-to-day reality and help men and fathers to be a resource for learning how to be better, loving, healthy fathers for our daughters. That's what matters.

Consider this statistic: "Many daughters aren't expecting much from their men these days, considering the fact that one-third to one-half of all adult women are beaten by their husbands or lovers at some time in their lives."[5] Research has proven that a woman's sense of self-worth is deeply rooted in the interaction between her and her father during the developmental stages of her life. According to another article, "Fathers will help their daughters develop aspects of self-image and what they come to expect from men, society and the world."[6]

Yet another area to be mindful of is how we treat and view our wives and how our young daughters perceive their parents' relationships. If husbands love and care for their wives, treat them equally and respect them, there's a good chance their daughters will look for and expect some of these very same characteristics in the males they date and marry. This includes the way fathers talk and interact with their wives. Our young daughters witness our behavior with our wives every day and gradually determine how a man should treat his wife, and in effect, determine how they will allow boys and men to treat them in the future.

To a great extent, because I was raised by parents who showed no love or respect for each other, I still struggle occasionally to communicate effectively and positively with my wife and have to work hard at it every day. The affectionate interaction that should take place between a husband and a wife doesn't come naturally to me, the way it would have if I were exposed to healthier parental role models while growing up. Because of this, I'm continually committed to working on improving in this area.

I'm divulging my family background for a couple of reasons: First, so other fathers can recognize that we're all human, we all have our strengths and weaknesses, and we all make mistakes. What's promising is that we can learn from our mistakes and keep trying to do better and improve. Second,

writing this is therapeutic and holds me accountable along with the reader.

CHAPTER 8
Abuse

This particular topic is one of the most important, if not *the* most important to understand and focus on as a father. Many of us automatically associate child abuse with either physical or sexual abuse. This chapter explores the many forms of abuse and their effects on our young daughters' lives.

It wasn't until about seven years ago that I myself finally understood and realized all the different forms of abuse, their causes, and effects. My improved awareness of them came from counseling sessions as well as reading and research. One book that had a big impact on me in terms of chronicling the different forms of abuse was *Home Coming, Reclaiming and Championing Your Inner Child,* by John Bradshaw. As I mentioned earlier, I grew up in a family where abuse was commonplace. I didn't recognize until later on that there are also many types of nonphysical abuse, all with the potential to severely scar a person for life.

The following are types of nonphysical abuse:

1. Neglect–Parents exhibit neglect when they send their children a clear message that they have little or no time for them. That is, parents just don't care or take interest in their kids' eating habits, education, appearance, hygiene, activities, or interaction with others. A classic example of neglect is children continuing to ask one or both parents to spend time with them, talk to them, play with them, or read to them, and the parents just never have the time. This occurs daily because parents are so busy or don't have their priorities in order. How sad! In this instance, fathers are sending their daughters the message that they're not important enough to spend time with. Think for a moment how your little girl must feel. Her father, the one who should love her the most, doesn't have enough time for her. How do you think that makes her feel? Most adults feel awful when neglected by loved ones, and we have the advantage of maturity and life experience. We also have the reasoning to distinguish between good and bad, right and wrong. Remember, as healthy, functional fathers we must make our young daughters a priority and continually show and tell them how important they are to us.

2. How we talk to and treat others–This is another type of nonphysical abuse we tend to forget about. As fathers, if we continually talk negatively, gossip, or berate our spouses and others around us, our daughters will think this behavior is normal and are likely to mimic these unhealthy habits. Again, as fathers, if we handle our anger and frustration by yelling, screaming, or degrading others, our daughters will likely mimic this behavior as well. If we continually use profanity or blame others for our mistakes, failures, and problems, once again, our young daughters will likely follow suit.

3. Who we subject our children to–Here's another form of nonphysical abuse that many of us forget could have a lasting negative effect on children. As fathers, if we make poor choices in the people we spend time with and expose our daughters to, we are, in essence, abusing them. This may sound harsh, even ridiculous at first, but let's explore it more. Say, for example, one of my choices for a friend happens to have abusive or addictive behaviors. Suppose I spend a fair amount of time with this friend, exposing my wife and young girls to him as well. During our visits with this friend, he drinks heavily and becomes verbally abusive to his wife and children and uses inappropriate language or behavior. Suppose further that because he's a friend, I simply laugh at all his inappropriate, dysfunctional comments and actions and explain to my wife and young daughters, "It's no big deal. That's just the way he's always been." Well, since I make excuses for this friend and condone his inappropriate behavior, I'm sending my wife and daughters a clear message that this friend's behavior is tolerable and acceptable. When in fact, it's not! Any sane father would remove himself and his loved ones permanently from this type of person and that type of environment.

Remember, abuse comes in many physical and nonphysical forms and can have lifelong consequences if it goes unchallenged, denied, or unrecognized. Don't end up regretting for the rest of your life something you, another family member, or a friend did or said in your daughter's presence.

The Facts

I always thought it would be helpful to be able to flip to a specific chapter or section of a book and access all the reference material in one place. Therefore, for your convenience I've listed below the statistics, research, surveys, and statements I've collected over the past several years that discuss the importance of a healthy, loving relationship between fathers and daughters. (Note, a few others are mentioned throughout the book.)

Although this book is based on my personal feelings, experiences, philosophy, and passions, I realize it's important to find out what other people think and feel, for the sake of comparison and so readers can distinguish between my input and tangible, quantifiable data. So here are some facts and opinions from experts, statesmen, and professionals.

Father Facts:
• 24 million children (34%) live absent their biological father.[7]
• Children who live absent their biological father are, on average, at least two to three times more likely to be poor, use drugs, to experience educational, health, emotional and behavioral problems, to be victims of child abuse, and to engage in criminal behavior than those who live with their married, biological (or adoptive) parents.[8]
• "Over the past four decades, fatherlessness has emerged as one of our greatest social problems. We know that children who grow up with absent

fathers can suffer lasting damage. They are more likely to end up in poverty or drop out of school, become addicted to drugs, have a child out of wedlock or end up in prison. Fatherlessness is not the only cause of these things, but our nation must recognize it is an important factor." [9]

• "The single biggest social problem in our society may be the growing absence of fathers and their children's homes because it contributes to so many social problems. Without a father to help guide, without a father to care, without a father to teach boys to be men, and teach girls to expect respect from men, it's harder."[10]

• A 1997 study of college-age women and their fathers, all from intact families, found that the daughters most likely to become depressed had fathers who frequently were insensitive, unaffectionate, and unavailable. They also felt a keen sense of unworthiness and guilt. Some daughters expressed their hunger in adolescence by becoming "boy crazy" or in adulthood by being drawn to men like dad. Daughters who had fathers they could count on were most likely to be drawn to men who treat them well.[11]

• Research has proven that a woman's sense of self-worth is deeply rooted in the interaction between her and her father during the developmental stages of her life. According to the same research in the article, "Fathers will help their daughters develop aspects of self-image and what they come to expect from men, society and the world."[12]

• "Stemming from a girl's sense of self-worth, the most prominent effect that a father has on his daughter lies in her need for affection."[13]

• According to research from fathers.com, if a daughter learns at home that she is accepted and appreciated for her personal qualities; she will be much less likely to feel the need to earn love from men through physical means.[14]

Impact of Divorce on Girls

• Using data collected from three generations from a large sample of largely working-class and middle-class families residing in Southern California, it was found that parental divorce increased the likelihood that a daughter's first marriage would end in divorce by 114%.[15]

• Using a sample of more than 1,000 college students, women with divorced parents were less likely to have a secure attachment style, more likely to have an avoidant attachment style, and were less idealistic in their romantic beliefs.[16]

• A study of 71 college students found that daughters from divorced homes had more relationship problems and higher levels of depression than sons whose parents had divorced.[17]

Family Time vs. Work Time

• "I think quality time is just a way of deluding ourselves into shortchanging our children. Children need vast amounts of parental time and attention. It's an illusion to think they're going to be on your timetable, and that you can say 'O.K. we've got half an hour, let's get on with it.'"[18]

• "Parents are too busy spending their precious capital–their time and their energy–struggling to keep up with MasterCard® payments. They work long hours to barely keep up, and when they get home at the end of the day they're tired. And their kids are left with a Nintendo or a pair of Nikes or some other piece of crap. Big Deal."[19]

• A national poll conducted asked the following question: "What do you feel is the most important thing a father should provide for his children?" The categories listed were 1. Money, 2. Time, 3. Discipline, 4. Spiritual support, 5. Emotional Support and 6. Play. The survey showed that approximately 60% indicated Time with children as the most important. Just to show how important most thought Time was, the next closet category was Emotional Support, with 17%.[20]

• Speaking of time, as most of us complain about not having enough time in the day to do everything we want, including spending time with our children, here are the results of a survey titled, "Our Wasted Time": We spend an average of 40 minutes each morning watching television and an average of 145 minutes or (2 hours and 25 minutes) watching television every evening.[21]

Sexual Activity

•"If our daughters are to flower, they need optimal growing conditions. Almost always this means being lovingly cared for by mother and father. It is from her mother that a girl learns to be a woman; it is from her father that she learns what to expect from men in the way of love and respect."[22]

•"Today with the rise in illegitimacy and divorce, fewer fathers are around to protect and defend their daughters' safety and honor. With more girls lacking the love and attention that only a father can give, more of them are willing to settle for perverse alternatives, namely, seeking intimacy with predatory adult men."[23]

•"Having loving parents you can talk to can help reduce teen pregnancy. Fathers [especially] are very influential in the decision to have sex."[24]

• 76% [of teenage girls] said that their fathers were very or somewhat influential on their decision to have sex.[25]

• "Teenage girls who grow up without their fathers tend to have sex earlier than girls who grow up with both parents. A fifteen-year-old girl who has lived with her mother only, for example, is three times as likely to lose her virginity before her sixteenth birthday as one who has lived with both parents."[26]

• "Girls who lived with their biological fathers throughout their lives, and whose fathers spent more time caring for them during the first five years of life, had later onset of puberty by the seventh grade. In contrast, daughters from homes where fathers were either absent or dysfunctional experienced puberty relatively early. Other research shows it is likely for girls with a highly involved, present-in-the-house father to begin sex and dating at a later age."[27]

• "The implications of this are scary. In a sense fathers teach their daughters how they should expect to be treated by males when they get older. They teach them by the way they speak and act toward them and through their treatment of the females, especially their own partners. The high proportion of girls who grew up with violent fathers who marry similar men or live in relationships with violent men is testament to the strength of this type of conditioning. The message for dads is simple–be gentle, be respectful and allow your daughters to be assertive towards you. There is increasing evidence to suggest that fathers are linked to the development of a girl's healthy self-esteem, particularly in adolescence. At a time when 60% of teenage girls have dieted, presumably in search of the perfect female figure presented in magazines, a father's positive comments may well make a difference to how his daughter sees herself. Reluctant as many dads are to compliment their daughters, positive comments about appearance and dress can be very reassuring. Most girls, like boys, still want their fathers' approval–although many don't know how to get it . . ."[28]

Diet and Body Image

• **Body Image:** 90% of all girls ages three to eleven have a Barbie Doll®, an early role model with a figure that is unattainable in real life. Or at age thirteen, 53% of American girls are "unhappy with their bodies." This grows to 78% by the time girls reach seventeen. And, 80% of 10-year old American girls diet. The number one magic wish for young girls ages eleven to seventeen is to be thinner.[29]

• A university study found that 90% of all female teenagers were unhappy with their weight.[30]

• 40% of nine and ten-year-old girls have tried to lose weight.[31]

Sex Education, Smoking, Drugs, and Alcohol

Well, here we go again, another section that's likely to be controversial. These are "hot-button" issues for society on many levels, since in one form or another they are related to money, power, religious beliefs, political views, morality issues, and addictive behavior, and people feel strongly about them. Rather than taking a hard-line, moral stance on either side of these issues, I promise to try to focus on how they can potentially affect our young daughters' lives.

Sex Education: Let's start with sex and how we approach the subject with our girls. First, it's important to do some research and consult with the professionals in this area so you know exactly what you should tell her, at what age, and how explicit you should be. Unfortunately, fathers, and others as well, often believe this fact-finding mission and follow-up discussion with their daughters are better suited for mothers. This is an area still steeped in traditional stereotypes and gender bias. That is, historically mothers would talk to their daughters, fathers to their sons. I completely disagree with that practice, and I suggest and encourage fathers to be involved with the entire process.

Here's why: The sooner a father connects with his young daughter, on all levels, the better. What better way is there to emotionally connect with her, show her she can trust you, and make her feel as if she can talk to you about anything, including sex? If she feels as if her father is committed to her education and fully aware of her sexuality, she'll feel more secure about herself when relating to other boys and men. As she gets older, she'll feel more comfortable coming to her father with sexual concerns, and even more important, she'll continue getting viewpoints from a man's perspective. That said, I realize there are times when our young daughters will feel more comfortable talking to their mothers about this topic as well as others. Some issues could be awkward or embarrassing for them and require a mother's specific viewpoint. That's normal and fine, but they should know they could always come to their fathers too.

Many of us mistakenly continue to shy away from the topic of sex or treat it as if it's forbidden or should be kept secret until a certain age. Of course, everything about this topic must be approached with caution, in stages, and at the proper ages. However, if we have wholesome, frank, but appropriate conversations with our young daughters instead of leaving them in the dark or forcing them to get the advice elsewhere, we'll have a better chance at relating to them successfully. My wife and I started with our daughters at about age seven, sitting down with them individually, drawing examples from books and other material to support the information we shared to assure that it was age appropriate. We continually schedule conversations with them, individually and jointly, and divulge more details as they both get older.

Besides individual discussions, we continually talk frankly with our daughters about sex on a number of different levels, depending on the situation. It might be as simple as chatting with them when they come home from school. One of our daughters might say to us, "Oh, she's boy crazy. All she talks about is boys and who she likes and who likes her."

In this case, we'd ask, "What do you think about that type of behavior?" and "What do you think boys might think about that type of behavior?" Then we would have a discussion about it and explain that there's absolutely nothing wrong with talking and thinking about boys. As a matter of fact, it's very normal. However, we'd explain that, as individuals, they need to work at being a complete person, respected and treated equally by both sexes and should also focus on schoolwork and other activities. In other words, it's normal and fun and exciting to think about boys, but they still need to spend time on all the other important things in life as well.

Let's say that one day our daughter comes home and tells us a boy at school said something mean or inappropriate about another girl's breasts. Once again, first we'd ask our daughter, "What do you think about that boy's comments, and how do you think it made the other girl feel?" or "What do you think about a boy who behaves that way?"

I hope my daughter would respond, "What he said was wrong, and it embarrassed her in front of her friends," and "I would never like a boy who says stuff like that or treats others that way."

Please note that during these hypothetical conversations with our daughters my wife and I never mention that the girl who was boy crazy or the boy who made inappropriate remarks were bad or terrible people. This is very important to remember when discussing others with your daughter, because the fault usually lies in the person's behavior or comment, not in the person. Does this make sense? If we focus on the person's behavior and the fact that it's inappropriate, unacceptable, or harmful rather than the person, it sends a better message. We'd explain to our daughters that saying and doing these things doesn't make these other children at school bad people, especially if they don't know any better. It just means they probably weren't taught to be kind or to respect other people or that possibly their friends are influencing them. We'd explain, "We just don't know the reason, but what we do know is that we don't want you to associate with other children like that as long as they continue acting that way or treating others that way."

Obviously, these are just a few examples out of hundreds of possibilities. Keep in mind that our daughters are eight and eleven. The topics that come up and the conversations that parents have with this age group are a lot different from those, say, with girls who are thirteen and sixteen. I'll close this topic by stressing two crucial points: First, we fathers really need to take our daughters' sex education seriously and be a part of the process from the very first discussion onward. Second, please work hard at being a good role model for your daughter, so she can hold you up as an example of how boys and men should act and talk around her and other females as well.

Smoking: I don't think anyone right now could make a case for the positive benefits or the effects of smoking, especially after the tobacco industry's recent admissions regarding the harm

smoking does to us and the multitude of law-
suits filed and won in courts across the country.
In spite of all this information about its negative
effects, smoking remains one of our most dangerous and addictive habits. It's bad enough that millions of people still smoke, but even worse, those
who smoke are also potentially harming and killing others around them who don't. I'm sure you
realize I'm talking about second-hand smoke. It's
deadly.

As fathers, since we are fully aware of the
dangers of smoking, we need to educate our daughters early on about these dangers and the effects
it can have on us. Awareness is the best chance
we have of keeping our daughters away from the
habit. Continually talk to them about the benefits
of keeping their bodies healthy and how smoking
can damage the lungs, heart, and other organs,
potentially making them sick no matter how hard
they work at staying fit.

Be aware that, as much as cigarette adver-
tising has been challenged and reduced over the
years, your young daughter will still be exposed
to subtle messages about how smoking is cool and
even glamorous. Of course, the most dangerous
sales pitch of all will likely come from her friends
and classmates. Peer pressure is a huge factor, and
typically the first reason any child tries smoking.
So, as much as possible, get to know your daughter's friends and those with whom she spends her
time. If parents themselves smoke or spend time
around others who do and condone it, there's a
greater chance that their daughters will experi-
ment with smoking sooner than later. It's a good

idea to share with your daughter some real life examples of people you know who have smoked and the suffering the habit has caused them. Be straightforward. Don't shy away from the fact that people get sick and die every day because of cigarettes, and there's nothing glamorous at all about it.

Drugs: As with smoking, we fathers really need to start talking to our girls as soon and as often as possible about drugs and the terrible harm they can cause. Remind them not only about the mental and physical damage drugs can cause, but that the major difference between doing drugs and smoking or drinking alcohol is that drugs are illegal. This means they have the potential to ruin their lives in yet another way; drugs can get them arrested. If they get arrested, it becomes part of their record, which stays with them for many years, possibly permanently.

These messages we send to our daughters don't have to be accusatory or delivered in a way that threatens them, but it should be made very clear how serious drug abuse could be. People get sick from them, become addicted to them, squander their money on them, and, yes, die from them. Your girls should know that people ruin their lives and the lives of others by taking drugs. Even experimenting with drugs can get you kicked out of school permanently, kicked off a sports team permanently, fired from your job, or can permanently ruin your career. Drugs can be devastating, as smoking and drinking alcohol can also be. The most important thing for fathers to continually tell their daughters is not to bow to peer pressure. I keep coming back to this issue of peer pressure. Sooner or later, your girls will likely be approached by peers who have experimented with drugs, cigarettes, and alcohol and who are looking for another "partner in crime."

Alcohol: Alcohol is probably the most challenging of these topics parents have to discuss with their daughters because it's legal, it's glamorized, it's used as a form of entertainment almost everywhere, and it's a staple in many households. The reality is that alcohol, when abused, is a terrible menace to society for a number of reasons. First, it causes physical and mental harm to millions of people, thereby ruining countless families, and it results in sickness and death. I have firsthand experience with this issue because my father was an alcoholic. He was sick, mentally, due to his addiction to alcohol and drugs. As a result, our entire family became dysfunctional and chaotic, which led to emotional and physical abuse and lifelong challenges for all of us.

Most adults drink alcohol every once in a while or have a glass of wine in the evening or a cocktail at a party. They might be very responsible about the way they drink. Does the fact that these people drink alcohol periodically and responsibly make them bad people or harmful to themselves or to society? Certainly not, and the majority of people would probably agree. So this is not about taking a moral stance or judging other people by whether they drink or not; it's about how each of us fathers needs to discuss alcohol consumption in a fair but serious manner with our young daughters. Take some time by yourself or with your spouse and decide how you're going to approach the subject. Be prepared for the questions that will most likely come up and have answers ready that will support your message. You're sure to get questions: "Dad, did you drink when you were younger?" or "Dad, why do you drink beer every once in a while?" or "How come there's alcohol at some of the parties we go to?"

These are all very good questions. As with cigarettes and drugs, make sure your daughter is fully aware of the potential harm drinking alcohol can cause her and others. Explain to her that in our society there are some questionable habits that are legal for adults, such as smoking at age eighteen and drinking alcohol at age twenty-one. Explain that the reasoning behind age requirements is that, as adults, we should be more capable of making wiser, more responsible decisions about these habits. However, point out that no matter our age, sometimes we still don't make wise, responsible decisions.

Explain that just as with drugs, minors can get into big trouble, including being expelled from school, sports, etc., if caught drinking alcohol. Fair or not, the same serious consequences could apply whether you've had just one drink or ten. Let her know, if she gets into a car with someone who has been drinking, and even if she hasn't been drinking, her life and the lives of others are at risk. Explain further that driving while under the influence of drugs or alcohol is illegal and punishable as a crime by law. Even worse, if a person were to be responsible for killing someone because they were driving while under the influence of drugs or alcohol, they could potentially go to prison for many years.

Last but not least, and as repetitive as it sounds, caution your daughter not to give in to peer pressure. Eventually, she'll be approached by friends and others who will encourage her to drink, and the better prepared she is to handle those situations, the easier it will be to say no or walk away from them.

To summarize the message in this crucial chapter on sex education, smoking, drugs, and alcohol: First, be well prepared for discussions with your young daughter regarding these topics. Second, remember that the detail and explicitness of your discussions depends on her age. Don't be afraid to get advice and help by reading books, consulting with family members and friends you trust, or professionals in the field. Third, and probably most important, try to conduct these discussions in a loving and caring manner, not in an accusatory or shaming way. We have a much better chance for a successful, meaningful dialogue with our daughters if our approach is adult-like and responsible.

CHAPTER 9
Rebuild your Relationship

As we come to the final chapter in this book, I felt it was necessary to spend some time talking to those fathers rebuilding relationships with their daughters—those fathers who unfortunately, for one reason or another, didn't get a chance to develop and establish a healthy, loving relationship with their daughters. In addition, this chapter is for fathers who had the chance but didn't take advantage of their time while their daughters were still young and now want to try to rebuild the relationship together. Let me say right up front, I applaud any father and give him all the credit in the world if he cares enough about his daughter to acknowledge he made some mistakes in raising her and now is determined to make amends. Certainly, none of us can change what happened in the past, but we can learn from it and change things for a better future. So let's talk about what we've learned and begin to work at improving as fathers and rebuilding a relationship with our daughters.

Suppose your daughter is now seven, twelve, sixteen, twenty-two, thirty-six, or maybe even fifty-four, and your relationship is strained or broken off. It really doesn't matter; what does matter is that as a father you're committed to change the situation. Of course, questions will immediately surface: What will your daughter think about this? What if she still harbors some anger or resentment, or what if she's just not interested? Then what does a father do? Well, there are many things a father can do to try to reestablish or start to build a new relationship with his daughter. I realize there could be any number of scenarios or variables surrounding what may or may not have happened between the two of you in the past, but I'll discuss and explore a few examples and offer suggestions as to how a father might make some progress.

First, it's critical that a father understands what it was he did or didn't do in the past to cause either a strained or broken relationship with his daughter. Once you know where you went wrong, it's clear you made mistakes in the past, and you feel remorse and regret for them, you're on the right track. You're on the right track because you're sincere about your feelings and regrets, and you feel badly enough about it to share it with the person you love, your daughter. Once you're ready to share your feelings with her, call her or write a letter, whichever you feel is more appropriate for the initial contact. If you call her, assure her that you really want to talk to her as well as listen to her, and you would like to meet with her. If you send her a letter, you might want to be a little more descriptive; convince her you know that you made some big mistakes in the past and would really like to talk to her about them and make amends. The way you handle this depends on the age of your daughter and the severity of the problems or the conditions surrounding your past relationship. Obviously, if your daughter is only seven years old and you're just now realizing that you need to make adjustments, the challenge and approach you face are simplified because she's still at home, I hope. However, if your daughter is forty-two with her own house, husband, and children, this presents a different challenge and approach.

If your daughter is still young and living with you, take the time to sit down with her on a daily basis and talk to her about your mistakes and regrets. Convince her you are committed to making changes because she means so much to you. Make yourself accountable to her and tell her exactly what you'll be doing differently than before and why it's important that you make these changes. Use this book as a resource to help research other options available to keep you on track. This far into the book, you should have plenty of ideas and information to draw from to help prove to your daughter that you really are making a change and a difference in your life in order to reestablish a healthy, loving relationship with her. Lastly, the most critical part of a second chance is that you make sure you respect the opportunity and work very hard at not slipping back into old habits and disappointing your daughter over and over again. Avoid back and forth empty promises and reaching a point where your daughter just doesn't trust or believe you any more. A letdown like that can leave her with lasting scars and permanently ruin things between you. If you're given another chance, please look at it as a blessing and try everything in your power to save and preserve that precious relationship.

If your daughter is an adult now and out on her own, as I mentioned earlier, your challenge and approach will be much different, not only because she doesn't live with you anymore, but also because she probably recognizes what she has missed out on by not having a good relationship with her father. She might also be informed enough to wonder if some of the choices she made in life involving the men she dated or married would have been different if her relationship with you had been better. She might wonder if her poor relationship with you had anything to do with the jobs she's had, the way she manages her finances, whether she decided to finish college or not, or whether she stayed in an abusive relationship.

These again are only examples, but real ones, the types fathers could face and will need to work through when trying to reestablish relationships with their adult daughters. It might not be as severe; it might be even more complicated or difficult. The bottom line is that no matter how difficult it is or the amount of time it might take, I encourage you to keep working at it, even if your daughter says she won't have anything to do with you. Keep writing her letters or calling, and make every effort at some small progress. As difficult and painful as it might be, you must understand that you can't expect your daughter to change the way she feels overnight, especially if you were absent physically and emotionally for the first fifteen or twenty years of her life. Please give it time and be patient. Know that however long it takes, it will be worth it in the long run.

You're the only father your daughter will ever have!

I thought this was an appropriate section title to end the book because it really says it all. There are so many important areas to focus on and be concerned about as a father. Yet in the end, the way your daughter lives her life could have everything to do with the type of relationship she had with you while growing up. This book focuses on the critical formative years of your daughter's life, between birth and the age of eleven. This period is so critical, because when your little girl is born into this new world, she has no expectations at all. The only things she needs from her father are love, protection, and time. Then as she gets to be two or three years old, she not only needs her father's love, protection, and time, she needs her father to play with her, and she needs him to provide structure and discipline and still more time with her.

At three or four years old, she needs all of the above plus even more of your time. She needs her father's companionship and involvement. At five or six years old, add to the list: support, guidance, teaching, and a positive role model. After this age, statistics show there's a very good chance your young daughter has already developed much of her character and biological blueprint. At seven to nine years old, her additional needs are leadership and for her father to demonstrate and talk to her about how boys and men should treat girls and women.

To summarize, by the time your daughter is eleven, she needs love, protection, playtime, companionship, involvement, support, guidance, teaching, leadership, for her father to be a role model and to demonstrate and talk to her about how boys and men should treat girls and women, and then some. So are you totally overwhelmed and exhausted yet? I am, just writing about the tremendous responsibility of raising a daughter and the overwhelming yet privileged task of developing a healthy, loving relationship with her. In case you're wondering why I stopped at age eleven, there are two reasons: First, to give you a chance to catch your breath. Second, because my oldest daughter is eleven now, and I have no experience or resources to draw from after this age. Sorry, fathers, I can't offer any help right now to those of you with teenagers.

See you in five or six years.

AUTHOR CONTACT INFORMATION:
www.healthylovingfathers.com
and 1–800–620–4345

ENDNOTES

[1] www.justthink.org- resources Brumberg, 1997

[2] Money Magazine (January 2005)

[3] www.careerjournal.com-By Jeffrey Zaslow (March 2004)

[4] www.justthink.org/resources/facts.html Pediatrics (2001)

[5] Patrick Crossland, October 31, 2003. Article: "Fathers be good to your daughters". www.collegian.com, www.take-backthenight.org

[6] According to the article, "When they need you most, dads and daughters" by Carma Haley Shoemaker.http://dadstoday.com/resources/articles/dadsanddaughters.html

[7] Father Facts 4th Addition 2002 (National Fatherhood Initiative)

[8] Father Facts 4th Addition 2002 (National Fatherhood Initiative)

[9] President George W. Bush, speaking at National Fatherhood initiativeís 4th annual national summit on fatherhood in Washington, D.C., June 7, 2001. Father Facts 4th Addition 2002 (National Fatherhood Initiative)

[10] Former President Bill Clinton, from a speech at the University of Texas, Austin, October 16, 1995. Father Facts 4th Addition 2002 (National Fatherhood Initiative)

[11] Father Facts 4th Addition 2002 (National Fatherhood Initiative)

[12] When they need you most, Dads and Daughters, Carma Haley Shoemaker http://dadstoday.com/resources/articles/dadsanddaughters.htm

[13] Patrick Crossland, Colorado State Collegian, October 31, 2003.

[14] www.fathers.com

[15] Feng, Du, et al. "International Transmission of Marital

Quality and Marital Instability." Journal of Marriage and the family 61 (1999) 451 463.

[16] Sprecher, Susan, Rodney Cate, and Lauren Levin. "Parental Divorce and Young Adultsí Beliefs About Love." Journal of Divorce and Remarriage 28 (1998): 107 120.

[17] McCabe, Kristen M. ìSex Differences in the Long-Term Effects of Divorce in Children: Depression and Heterosexual Relationship Difficulties in the Young Adult Years.î Journal of Divorce and Remarriage 27 (1997): 123 134.

[18] Dr. Ronald Levant, as citied by Laura Shapiro, "The myth of quality time," Newsweek, May 12, 1997.

[19] Harvard Psychiatrist Robert Coles, 1991.

[20] The National Fatherhood Initiative and www.fatherhood.org

[21] By John MacIntyre, Our Wasted Time - Special to the Mercury News, February 27, 2005 Market Probe International

[22] Evelyn Bassoff, PH.D, "Cherishing our Daughters": How parents can raise girls to become strong and loving women, 1998.

[23] Gracie S. Hsu, "Leaving the vulnerable open to abuse," Perspective, September 9, 1996.

[24] Survey of teenage girls conducted by Mark Clements Research, as cited in Parade, February 2, 1997.

[25] Clements, Mark. Parade, February 1997.

[26] Smith, Lee. "The New Wave of Illegitimacy." Fortune 18 April 1994: 81ñ94.

[27] Published in the Journal of Personality and Social Psychology and conducted by Vanderbilt, Auburn, and Indiana Universities.

[28] www.positivepath.net by Michael Grose, a parenting and work | life balance specialist.

[29] www.justthink.org resources- Brumberg, 1997.

[30] www.dads-daughters.com -Absentee Fathers: The cur-

rent State of Fatherhood - Study conducted by the University of Arizona

[31] An ongoing study funded by the National Heart, Lung and Blood Institute. (USA Today, 1996)

Contact Joe Cucchiara or order more
copies of this book at

TATE PUBLISHING, LLC

127 East Trade Centre Terrace
Mustang, Oklahoma 73064

(888) 361 - 9473

Tate Publishing, LLC

www.tatepublishing.com